The GEOMETRY of FREEDOM

AFTERNOON BOOKS | NEW JERSEY

Copyright © 2016 by Afternoon Books

All rights reserved. Any resemblance to actual people, living or dead, or to businesses, companies, events, institutions, or locales is coincidental. No part of this publication may be reproduced, distributed or transmitted in any form or by any means without prior written permission.

Designed and published by Afternoon Books, New Jersey, USA
Visit us online at www.afternoonbooks.com
All correspondence should be directed to publisher@afternoonbooks.com

The Geometry of Freedom / Henry Cunningham. – 1st ed.
ISBN 978-0-9974885-0-0
eBook ISBN 978-0-9974885-1-7
Library of Congress Control Number 2016905799

In the bottle the recipe brews,
Its stuff is the shape of the shadow in the mirror,
Fueled by fire and the lotus flower, they are the same,

And in the middle turns the wheel
with perfection for its architecture,
Swimming and spinning forever
among the bubbles and currents,

All the while the geometry of freedom
forges its design in our heads and hearts,
Its nature is fluid, its path lies underfoot,
Burning for realization
and Being
as We do.

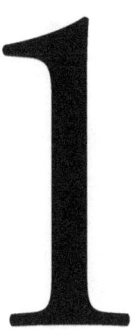

The Seed opens by the might inside,
The Heart ignites with the taste of light,
The Road beckons with hungry horizons,
Our Eyes all wet and bright.

One Little Victory in Eternity

Hallelujah! Praises be! I am free! I am free!
And my dreams are full of reverie!
Let my insatiable reverie overwhelm me!
Let my dreams explode with impossible closeness!
Let my dreams dissolve with the unnecessary!
Let the world sparkle through my eyes
shimmering with amazing Melody
like liquid Light all through my veins
and overtaking my hopes with the hardness of reality!
Let the Breeze of relief put giants on their knees,
quell the lungs and buzz the bees!
Let this poem burst from the page
and explode your brain with magnanimity!
Let this poem be read slowly,
it is made out of Bliss which in any dose runs swiftly,
Let the ways of pain take hoisted masts
to go ahead and sail away!
Let them sail forever on oblivion seas
and their seasons be turned by the saving grace,
Let the wisdom of a hint and a smile
abolish the seeds of stale beliefs!

Hallelujah pull the curtains down!
Hallelujah let the Songs be sung!
Om Mani Padme Hum!
Om and Hallelujah as One!
Hallelujah smash the rungs of confusion and distraction!
Hallelujah let praises be for all our little stings and
maiming wounds of the heart and mind!

Hallelujah for wishing next time
to go free from the start without all the hurt!
Hallelujah in the foxhole!
Hallelujah in the empty void of existence for its own sake!
Hallelujah for the harmonious purposes
intertwined as surprises
with all the ones we make and fake!
Hallelujah for the impervious Mystery,
the ever unknowable that we must seek!
Hallelujah for our limitless dreams
and this Dream of being in a universe of its own meaning!
Hallelujah let the Golden Lesson only go realized
and learned with the pangs of disappointment
and all our cares kicked to the dirt!

Let the Growth come from the Gut inside!
Let the Fruit come flying out through all routes!
Let the daring dreamers crash down the ceiling!
Let the flying feet not forget the ground
and the head never duck beneath the clouds!
Graces be to those who seek, may they sing Hallelujah
and see their dreams alight with reverie!

Hallelujah cannot heal the hurt or blow the storm away,
Let the Sound and the Suggestion of amazing Mirth
come from the one who listens and sings
and sees himself the same!
Hallelujah means thanks to the One, praises to the One!
Hallelujah to the One who needs no praise,
it is ours alone to somehow feel closer!
Hallelujah the closeness we seek is closer than we think!

Hallelujah to the Original Dreamer!
Hallelujah to the Maintenance Maker!
Hallelujah to the Everything Taker!
Hallelujah to all transformations
set in motion to something other!
Hallelujah for all the same stuff in different configuration!
Hallelujah there is no destruction only transformation!
Hallelujah there is no corner of the Dream undreamed!
Hallelujah every corner of the Dream unfolds!
Hallelujah to the Wheel and the River
and the Drum and the Space in Between!
Hallelujah to the Place from which all have come
and all will go, that is no place
and every place and forever Unknown!
Hallelujah to the Engineer of trees and stars
and the quantum and beyond!
Hallelujah to the Imminent Heard,
the Transcendent of Religion and Word!
Hallelujah to the Source!
Hallelujah to the Harbinger of Love!
Hallelujah to the Lifebreath of this Dreamworld!

Let the weights fall from the word
and make it new for the first Hallelujah!
Let the distractions dissolve
when we hum our mighty Om!
Let the Word reach beyond all names and phrases,
all thoughts and opinions, all skepticism, all devotion,
and all discernible notion! Om!
Let the ways inward go intersecting,

Each made from the other
Like the lightning that strikes
our Qualms and our Psalms into Nothing!
Let us see our World always in Freedom!
Let us see ourselves already Liberated
and use our Time to always Be!
Hallelujah I am Free!
You are Free!
Let our dreams be full of reverie!

Notes to Welcome a Dawn

Good morning to the sleeping birds and blooms,
Morning to the waiting trees,
The last of evening dissolves
too early and too late even for a passing breeze,

All abides its routine,
All arrives from its own stillness
the same for a regular day yet to begin
charged with the vapors
that saturate the promise of immanent change,
each day a regular one,
with no separation between any of them,

Look at those hues that emerge from an indeterminate
newness, from a chance to taste the brewing potential,
Look for the legs to carry every coming situation with the
rightness of mastery and the openness of humility,
Look for the road to reconcile imaginations of wildness
born with wiser deliverance from the rising
with the natural equity of compromise,
Look for the will to wonder freely on the origins of dreams
and configure them to perfect extremes,
Let go and take for fuel the product that remains,
Harvest wishes for guidance when needed,
Dig for the reserves to go forever forward
with errorless purpose and maximal absorption,

Mastery is burning the Stuff to be exuded on the day,
Mastery is being ready before the need emerges,

Good morning to the budding ideas and songs,
Morning to the single,
Morning to the throngs,
Good morning to the coming rights and wrongs,

Here's to washing our gears and hands
in the pristine perfection of the blank page of the day,
Here's to absolving neighbors without discretion,
To always being what can only be between moments,
To boosting our brighter intentions
before surrender sets in,
for the ephemeral present always giving opportunity,
Endlessly
for our Gliding,
for our Swimming,
for our Riding,
for our Going,
One dawn to the next
And all those to come beyond us.

To Glowing Ghosts in Living Dreams

A circle of friends with our forks and qualms
and our half glasses held ahead of our hearts
for a silent salute to the wavering and unsteady,

May we always be vital
and never trust the loafers to liberate ourselves alone,
May we give Cheers when we can
to let our palates gone dry be made wet
with the unity and the light just ahead of our eyes
Every one of us,
That is why we give Cheers, if only to say this once aloud

Here is to the ever-loving sea of gracing Milk
whose vastness is measured by eternity
and whose impossible depth is fully ablaze!
Let us always be the ever-loving mighty and puny!
Let us realize this vow when we give each glass a raise,
We rabble of blood oath companions,
May we each go now to journey onward!
May every star light up our hearts at night,
May we balance songs with books and burn the sounds,
May we peer with peace upon whatever lies ahead,
May we find light in our lives like wiser children today,
May we always be overflowing,
May we light each other's way.

Meteors for the People

Listen, hear the tune
The speed of light whistles by our eyes
but not so quick as the stuff of smiles,
Who could map the pace of gleaming clarity that washes
our feelings into oneness with a brilliant Creator,
a pervading Sustainer and a necessary Destroyer
come to float a breeze in your ear when even your heart
quiets a moment to hear it,

The Knight gave his salute
to reveal his presence without distraction,
the Soldier to show his preparedness for action,
the Civilian to tip the hat in courtesy,
the Artist to shield the sun and see more clearly,
the Stargazer to peer further into the endless evening,

Tonight the stars don't budge worth a breadcrumb
and by their light I offer this loving Thought to you
for the least our efforts can have us do,
You will choose Ignorance or a Song,
Together we will wonder
about when to stay and when to move on,
We know second chances seldom arrive again,
But new opportunities are as abundant
as the twinkling suns that surround us,
So let them all be in our paths and our chores,
Let them be forged and forgotten
and arrive sometime out of nowhere
as burning reminders of the need for open minds.

The Human Identity Mixology

I am ivory, I am bronze, I am copper,
I am ochre, I am honey, I am mahogany,
My recipe remains at the perfect levels
for the land where my ancestors rose,
like the plants and bears and dogs and deer and birds,
all rewarded for survival with the right formulation of their
design, as Nature's regards for a chance to make it there,
How essential that I preserve the pure essence of those
components that make the color of my identity special and
virtuous of itself,
How necessary that I integrate those special bits of myself
with the colors of all people who aren't the same as me,
How to balance the independence of identity
with the integration of humanity,
How to keep my colors from washing out
beyond recognition,
How to give my colors for others to share
and enjoy their gifts, preserved and evolving all at once,
How the definition of being ivory, bronze, copper, ochre,
honey and mahogany changes with the running river,
with the collective currents of living,
What part of this is the vehicle I've been assigned,
What part of this is irrelevant to the end game,
What part of this is necessary
for my freedom from the wheel of destiny
and what part connected with the backspin of fate,
What part of purpose depends on color,
What purpose for anything in a colorless world.

For the Invincibles

On growing up and the direction to guide it,

The direction to defy suggestions from those arrived,
realizing eventually that none have arrived,
That there is no place to arrive
and no satisfaction to be had,
but help can still be real
and we never know if it will, in advance,

Seldom knowing when or where, but going anyway,

And the surprise progress, the risen will,
grows out and grows in all at once,
The will dissolves and integrates and learns to focus,

For all that building and transfiguration,
What are the ways of truth for a man, for a woman,
The decisions of artistry and the crafted self,
The admissions of the liberating spirit
despite all the aspirations and illusions,

This one is for the invincibles
to hold steady the ways of goodness and daring,
to let space for the wild and the windblown,
to run and rest without thinking,
Ever with the will to stand without fear of sinking,
Ever to rise like buried treasure and stand again.

Hmm Hmm Hm

I hum a song I heard this morning
driving around town
blessing everything in the bright mid-morning,

I hum it and wonder about all the tough or fleeting loves
that have been had and hoped for,
aqueducts of the wishes that gleamed,
each one at its peak, and how we celebrated its eminence,

Humming this tune, I rain down on the afternoon all my
biggest sweetest praises to the loves I've known or passed
on the street, or met once in a blink,
or devote myself to with a way of living that grows,

Unbroken is the binding, the connection
saturating us through our shells and rinds and all,
To those I've been wrong and unkind, I apologize,
To those who wonder if that person you remember
sometimes ever thinks of you after all this time,
They do.

We can't reclaim the feelings that have been,
We let them go and remain open for new ones,
We don't have to be musicians to make some whistling
lips or dancing hips or concertos on the park bench,

Hum a tune and savor the pieces of days that find you free
enough to glide around in the lightness of reverie,
All our wishes and all our chances live in that melody.

For Witnesses and Wanderers
(And Those Who Don't Love You)

Once you start recalling the sunnier moments
then come too all the in betweens,
then the separation and the otherness is revealed
so much clearer now to see the Once that was,
All the way back to the meeting, that first time
the obvious and the impossible smashed together,
Your hesitations were from recognizing
some fundamental reflections,
when time stepped out of bounds for a moment
and each of you was introduced through the other
to a fullness known only to have been waiting,

In that moment went every loss and every whim
and every thing forever been up to then,
each of your mettles stretched immediately across its own
terrain to find that wobbling, that wandering,
that stumbler in the dark
whose path reaches back to find the rest of itself
and some forgotten pieces again,

The quiet, the unthinking, the apparent
shines a road ahead with no horizon and no bends
but perfect sight of that immediate underfoot,
that wild wonderful unknown,
Certain enough to dance upon,
it carries you through the acclimation
with an underlying awareness
that finds its fate as any comet might,

Hovering in your hands,
Yours to inform you,
Yours to maintain,
Here is where we see ourselves,
Here is where we discover our trade,
In all the findings, all the allowances,
the willful compromises and wiser concessions,
the asking, the confessions and the discoveries
of those same feelings grown and arrived somehow new,
the fuel of that great rekindling to carry the two as one,
orbiting their own singularity without diluting each other,

The momentum does not waiver from the inconveniences
or even the hardships of living,
but by some unspoken seed
lying all the while so deep beneath
that not until a certain restlessness
and some of these ingredients get cleaned
does it rear its head and belly and can never be unseen,

The sharing within one
becomes the exchanges between two again,
Where that extra light that was half reflection
and half come out from inside,
that glow from behind your eyes,
is now suddenly too far gone
from ever coming fully back again,
and only suggested to have ever been
by the wistfulness of a memory left behind
to catch up on its own,
By time stepped again out of bounds,

There are lapses and distractions and mistakes,
But for the slight of love
observed in the enduring thoughtfulness,
Lack is not an accident for them that go ahead
without turning aside, when once they did,

All these symptoms and vacancies
are not rightfully forgiven as subtleties,
But all that remains the opposite of these
is well known to the witness and to the wanderer
as that one thing,
if it could be real,
and to share in it,
anyone would dare to reach out and taste it,
and anyone can smell it already in the air.

Only the Necessary Sentiments

Who really cares for a passing into despair,
the shock of its arriving and sinking
from the trigger and the slip,
the plunge and absorption into its false offering,

Oh what is this that life has become,
Oh what should I do, what have I done,
How wonderful, how amazing
the memory of suffering
and the sweet moments I never realized until now,
How did I let them fall from bliss
when I was in the moment,
How can I return to the sublimity of how I used to be
when all of life was a rhyme as I remember it
and all of life was mine in the moment,
mine of the coming,
mine all laid out spread out waiting,
the inexhaustible and ready forever,
How cruel and uncaring the cold now comes
to leave me here despairing in so many pieces
and each one ready for surrender

But for some little part refusing,
knuckling down to drive right through
and tear down the walls
and burn the curtains of doubt for that confidence
that had welled up so easy and clean,
of doubting the victories that have been,

Was it all a sham, was it all illusion,
or this unbuckling,
this universe unraveled,
Is this the flipside that lay waiting,

What despair can make me better and take me there,
What despair can clean out the clocks in my hair,

No despair but the muscle to overcome,
No despair but the going anyway
No despair but the self-made motivation,
No despair but the levity and to give it some,

No matter the trying, no matter the abiding,
No matter the elements of man and fate
that may fly against the day,
All of this is fuel already and gone away

Oh what was that despair,
that imbalance of my bearing and gravity,
that distraction from the fairgrounds of the way.

The New Memory, One for the Weary

When you are running to everything
and everything has fatefully gone in the other direction,
When the last comfort has long since given satisfaction,
When all falls short and everything else is disgusting,
When no one seems caring enough
even for dismissal or some friction,
When virtues are the luxuries of the unexposed or the
endangered innocent, and cuteness is the mask that
lubricates fate's inevitable reckoning into pollution,
Stark and bare comes everything in the searching gaze,
Sharp is every corner, all vision seems free of even the
helpful veils but all the ingredients and outputs from the
day are convoluted and refuted,

All is tasteless, All is faceless,
All the ways and things left shining on the shelf are the
most precious goals, the greatest aspirations,
They have displaced all the tangible and the thoughtful
and the caring laid straight ahead just for you,

Swelling forever, pressure heats the ice from inside,
Slowly the fangs draw from what was forgiveness,
Lowly the fuel skews that kept simpler smiles
so close to surfacing for any old reason,
Impossible the fruit of opportunity to grow,
Swelling forever, disappointment exceeds its limits,
nothing left to strike down in the street
or throw or wipe or cast aside,

Hands have dirtied the pants and friends and faces
in their grasping for some fresher stuff to bring along,

Stolen together, the searched for and the searcher
are found emptier than naked and already seen through
as gone without a glimpse or a footprint,

The forest is empty
The road is threadbare
The shapes and objects from the hopes that replaced the
rest are rushed upon and mutilated in the tasting,

What then is left to stare upon,
What then is left to deflect the despair so much weight
was balanced on,
What then is left to soothe the forever unsettled
underneath whose reason is now ruined and grieved
and whose pitted boon is all that is left beside you
in your little room,

There is only one door open now to pull the whole
structure in, the lean-to architecture spit together with
venom and whims,

There is one door open somehow, not of the making
but for the spaces between your pushing and taking
and it shines its light in every corner,
Eventual surrender
is what lifts your vision from never-minding,
Eventual surrender
whispers hints of the dismantling and the reconstitution,

Silence in the sudden breeze that trickles in like water
tinkling in newfound paths,
and Silence in the leaves and pollen that spins around your
swollen head and stiffened hands,
and Silence in the rags and remnants of final chances given
up and given in,
and Silence in the surrender that all along had to come
eventually,
and Silence stirs in tighter swirls with suggestions of
something ready now to come,

But there is Nothing

What the world brings too when you bring the same,
The same a stranger gives to notice you,
All the world has more purpose,
more attention and interdependence,
You are the washed upon the shore,
released by a departed ocean,
ignored by the scavengers, like before and always,
a reflection with more interest than its source,
and turning in, looking out

Clouds over buildings
and hovering over spots on sleeping fields,
Blades of grass, and in between them,
underneath and high above
the machine of survival and sustenance turns somehow,
And you, and I, doing nothing, being nothing,
stopped and paused and set aside
not to rejoin but to enter anew,

And the door is open,

We, pulled in, and through, and ready
And in the stillness, still Nothing,
But the first pause
the fjord thought enters in
and already begun
jostles among a space in the certainties

        and then the Atom

                *

    its center and its stuff inside
  spinning little clouds with innumerability
     all its parts in every cell and cranny

  You can feel them, where are they all going!

And then the eyes surrender from looking,
the hands hold out steady as hearing,
the lifting head finds bugs lit up in flight
all golden in the dusty sunstream spilling out on your path
and everywhere in between,
and all of this inside you, you remember,
How life had to start small from the beginning,
those initial inventions born of themselves
and the chemistry and the asteroid crust
that made everything and will outlive all the rest,

So must we do the same in our time,

Give it all up!
Admit to all we've done!
Forgive, Forget, make our own Peace and then Go on!
I forgive myself! Go forgive yourself!
I absolve everyone and ask forgiveness!
Opportunities wasted can be forged again!
Every moment is every piece of every atom
and all the forces that make it all go!

We have passed through the portal before and so we step
forward to another new one, there is no fear!
There is no consequence
but the judgment we create on our own!
Go! Go! Go!
Go for the reason that brought you here!
Go for the reason that you're reading this little poem!
Go for freedom from reasons but that of its own doing!

What a relief the letting go, the giving up,
the breathing in, the purging out,
the new focus, the fueling clarity!
The effortless, the ease!
The disintegration of those that caused some heaviness to
begin with, some unfulfilled, some absorbing expectations
like the absence of light from its pulling in and crushing
from the sucking in to some forever necessary blackness!

Let it go! Bye bye!

There's nowhere that can't be part of this same
somewhere,

Every dimension and every layer of being
just needs a couple steps back
to see it's still part of the same everywhere that is Here!
Every dimension
pervades the anywhere there would be to run to!
What a relief!
We are already there!
So let's go do what's next for us
discovering again the meaning,
Illuminating or abandoning the enduring or useless
reasons,
Those we choose or let loose is who we'll be today,
Remembering to remember the place we originate inside
while we continue on to find the horizon up ahead,

If we can see it, we can be it,

Let's go make new memories
just so we can burn them up and make room for more,
because we choose to get up and do it,
because we can make a little something from what's gelled
up in these footprints once in a while,
and maybe sometime someday
we'll find we had been wandering
straight up to our own Enlightenment!
We can only make our own path,
We can only do it our own way,
We can be mindful of our footsteps without worrying over
the spaces in between and if they were alright
and what shape the next one should be,
All the right footsteps come from the machine inside,

We can go because we are composing our own stories
along the way, nevermind how much is left to be written
or where it goes with all the paths spun off from reading,
We can be our own stars
and let our light brighten the shadows of others,
We can choose to tread a path of liberation
from the heaviness and the weight,
And in making that path
that may be the destiny of any human being,
We can create a new memory
that doesn't need motivation or inspiration,
but of our own,
And to make our dark days
into treasures for plundering when we're weary,
into fuel for burning
and growing stronger from the incineration,
And our every day is another opportunity,
because we know nothing ever ends,
We know there is no time to make us too late
to own ourselves and let ourselves go at the same time,
and we know what that means.

*

The Bringer of News

Our Memory is greater than what we forget or remember,
It is ours alone to access but not ours to possess
and its fruits require no summons of vanished senses,
How have you come here,
How many decisions and footsteps are yours,
the purposeful and the accidents and the fortunate,
Do you taste our breaths and our dreams
swimming in the shared air,
Do we share a duty not to let our radiance overwhelm its
purpose, but to guide ourselves in peace or in play,
To ride our wills entwined with each dream's origin and
destiny,
To ride our fates connected by weightless visions like
springboard bridges of spontaneous making,
To ride along and imagine the ever loving Memory,
the forever tag-a-long,
absorbed and saturated and gone in the dissolved revelry,

Our Forgetfulness,
the intangible transformation of the faceless,
the incinerated archive of some moment's perfection,
dragged back by sparks of the unknowing
as propped up piles of bones,
Bones enough to wish for the taste
of some gone perfection again,

Do the gone moments lie in wait for secret resurrections,
Do the untapped memories disappear forever
in some permanent nonexistence

or hide away yet in impossible reserves,
Amid all our searching, our haunting,
our connection with gone moments,
what next ones wait to come springing up
and just as soon get burned to vapors
giving way to whatever transformation
or revelation might be ignited,

How many or how much of them are integrated already or
born of those that came before

Every time some lightning idea strikes
to bring us the news,
Was it born as a novel addition to the world,
Did it come from some resurrected bones of a moment
originated long ago whose ripples appear new,
Did the radiance of the decision and the dream
emanate from a reason
ready to be the footprints and the fuel,
And all the new ones soon to be
or riding quietly all along
So quickly become the fate of Memory again.

The Ego Protects the Ego

Defining Love for one's Self
is the only way to be able to share in it,
even before the offering and accepting
and growth beyond a need for its duality,
To love oneself, to hate oneself,
to find the whole conversation unworthy of the time,
All of these mechanisms are the constructions inside
perpetuating themselves as required by their origination
and encouragement,

There is a sensation with a singular receptor in the head or
the heart or the gut or everywhere throughout,
for that resonance, that connection that enlivens and
nourishes the fuel for what we are seeking,
How it feels is no confusion, when to point it out by name
is another situation, but what to do with its work and its
products is left for definition by the user,

The seasons of dissatisfaction, the routine of complaint,
how many times and cycles until the spirit inside lets in
the idea of freedom, the ridiculous dream,
the imagination untethered for a moment
with its fences laid flat by the sickness of repetition,

Only then can come the pursuit of breaking out,
And where to begin but with the impulses welling up
from underneath or automatic on the treadmill,
Where do they come from, why do they persist and how
much strength can they amass in their momentum,

To send the whole vehicle barreling down the mountain
without anyone to remember when and why
and how it started rolling in the first place,

True pursuit of providing one's own navigation
requires the driver to want something different
from what's always been done,
something more difficult and fruit-bearing
than the confusion of pride and being offended
with the autonomy of self-definition and insubordination,

The pursuit of liberation must be committed in full with
the patience and persistence of a stepwise approach, and
with the urgency of the thirst and the hunger that ravage
the nourishing fuel and ignore the inconsequential,

To forge incremental understandings of the mechanisms
inside, to reinforce conviction through one's attempts to
make it real, knowing the pursuit alone cannot lead one
into freedom,

The path then with no horizon becomes the sun shining in
one's world, the only blown shades from its grace are those
shackles to be figured out and dissolved to their undoing,

If one can imagine and conjure up Love
to live through their flowing days,
where else can the shackles originate but from one's own
imagination and conjuring just the same, and the pursuit
of freedom has become liberation from one's self,

To believe there is one of a few ways for the choosing
may provide a temporary stepping stone,
but these constructs are only bridges
that dissolve with the crossing,
From now to the everlasting, the vehicle will be
abandoned when the driver realizes one's own limitless
power and crafts a vessel of the self for its passing,

Then begins the braveness of the diving,
the confrontation of the conniving,
the pursuit of the origins of every derivation,
the opening up from shedding dead weights
in closer approximation to the center of the source,

Along this path the barriers stand like pines
to mask sunshine from the way,
They are not the ones spun from others or given off
by fates resounding with echoes through our day,
The barriers are projections set to hang with weights
we assign to ties we believe to be the things
keeping us from shining,
We are all that stands in our way,
We are all that shines and all that casts a shadow on the
path, and our journey begins with mastery of the ego,
which has entrenched itself in protection of the ego,
But we are the thorn and the wound,
We are the journey and the road,
We are the sword and the shield and the song,
We are the seekers of our liberation, however long.

Admission &

Take it all away from the fortunate daughters and sons,
take it all away from their unfortunate compadres,
from those born into abuse, war and poverty,
take it away from the victims of a prejudiced majority,
take it away from the disabled, the maimed,
the badly changed, and their families,
take it away from the unprotected sufferers of another's
beleaguered state, the neglected, the self-defeating,
and the tortured minds of tyranny,

Go on a journey with all the questions
of the wandering spirit and its desperation for a reason
Why,

First she asks her Lover or her Mother, how can this be,

Next to the Friend or the Neighbor, how do bad things
happen to good people, and fortunes fall upon the unjust
like water,

Dissatisfied, he turns an eye to his Government or that of
a prominent land, how could you let us down and why did
you bring only a heavy hand instead of what we needed,

With no redeeming information, she appeals to the stars
above and the hearts in love, why couldn't it have been
different for him or for me, or the others I see in tragedy,

Desperate for something, and fully unanswered, he asks
finally of the God in between,
how can you let all these nightmares and destruction be,
why do you not lift a finger to intervene,

And all reply in silent unison,
with no spectacles or miracles, that the living is hard,

Finally, broken from exhaustion of all sources around,
she finds one last place left on the shelf,
there all the while but just now appeared,
she asks of the Self, why do no others have tangible
answers for me, where is the place that I need to be,

And the Self replies

What troubles are these you consign and prescribe,
they are the pieces of your life that have brought you to
this very place, and each in theirs to abide,
You are alone in space,
You are surrounded in space,
You are one blink of a little something amidst everything,
And each thing you identify is the same little blink as you,
Made of all the same stuff,
You and the space are all as One,
What separation is there from the being that singles out
suffering and gives it a fountain for overflowing,
Ask better yet what are the symptoms
of that which constrains your illuminated self,
your enlightened mind, that is no mind, but Being,

Such that none can touch you, but you are not cold,
None can hold you down, but you are not closed,
None can hurt you
but what reflection of the offender you let inside,
You are not victorious,
You are not beaten,
Only let yourself be wild
and thrive enough to design your own transformation,

The chains are mine but the Voice is yours,
Free yourself from the questions with no answers,
Free yourself from your reliance on Me
and replace that spiral of despair with a spark in your will
to do something that needs doing
for the better of all the saints and pirates
that you see in your reflection,

Set yourself on a path worth fighting for
with no expectation of an end,
no comfort and no torture,
Set yourself on a journey with no horizon,
and work will find your hands,
love will find your friends,
liberation will rise from your dead ends,
and keys will be forged for all of your questions.

Forever Adolescence Blues

Which are the ways of youth
whose sense is right and fresh,
The uncorrupted insights
giving lifebreath again to everlasting ways,

Which are the ways of youth
whose ambitions overwhelm the substance underneath,
whose ideas are less the arrivals of wisdom
than the shadow of having discovered anything at all,

Which are to be savored and nurtured and preserved,
Which to be identified and shaved and catapulted,
Which are the tools that help us
to tell the difference among them,
Which are the moods that cloud our judgment,
Which aesthetics of thinking survive the clearing out
of exposure and experience and time,
Which are left ahead to be imagined and remembered,
What do they look like
and how to know them from the substance of being,

Which are the ways of youth so bright and weightless
and impermeable and burning
as the source of the will to ask these questions.

For Those with Brains and Backbones

Do our brains always guide us
to what is right and best for us,
and if not every time, then which,

This is the handicap to offset our cognitive capacity
even for the tools and skills we cultivate
that our neighbors in the kingdom do not,
We remain woefully limited in our collective throws,
though the individual has everything
that is needed to try and to thrive,

Here is our nature,
to follow this but not that
and to ride the road that lies ahead
from the decision or the accident, to continue on,
to go with the gut or mull it over,

Besieged by ideas,
Freed by ideas,

Driven by the source that generates all impulses,
all measured thoughts, all brilliance and all speed bumps,

Is fate so entwined that our brains always guide us
to what is necessary
or just what is available,
but for the unaccounted element,
the secret ingredient that exists only to break through,
to bust out, to try something new,

If only this was unique to us,
we could claim that all the things our brains discriminate
are not made of the same stuff,
And that we are not sharing and struggling
in the same indiscriminate venue.

Practice

For the might of the newfound growth—

The kite and the air and why not,
May labor and I absorb the scents of the rest,
of the most and the just right
in a song in time to ride upon,
Oooooh it's the branches in tangles
for grace and persistence through the night
and the bloooooo day
where we sing Geronimo! for surrender
and take our wine or water or plain old repose
in the shade, making love out of any old thing,
taking laughs from our worst memories
Because we are the volunteered condemned,
the self-made rebellious,
We are the deciders of our balance
and we can do anything with a decent flock of reasons,
the blood from inside
helping shape our hearts all over our faces

For the fight of the rising lowest—

The wheel and the road and we two,
My labor and I spend our summers in the garage,
autumn in the shed,
winter in the basement,
and spring the shed again,
Whooooa-ho-ho take your wishes down from the eaves
when the creaks keep you up

and you know how they grow so slow into dreams
with distinct dimension and color
their little metaphysical lives
and you ring for fulfillment and liberation
in the same wild sigh, the same silent try,
Because we are the engineered perplexed,
the well-tooled coincident,
We are the repliers to our questions
and we can fool anyone with a hang-up for the seasons
and make floods of the tides
telling tales of the runners and the races

For the plight of the departing loved—

The picture and the smell and the smile,
Labor's remains and I continue to look for the best,
with none to come better than what we'd done,
Heyyyyyy what's that newwwwws you heard the world
blow whoa-ho, didn't you already know you're as much
the same as how you've changed, until the last guess to
come from your chest when all the hues and all the fuel
disintegrate in freedom leaving the rest
to notice everything around you going on without delay,
Because we are the indigenous impermanent,
the some-time ratified,
We can be the stuff we can't touch with inventions
and shake doves through the night
with ourselves meant to wake and rise
and sleep the dreamless integration
with what we'd sought and ignored all the while
as our perfection.

No Revelations Tune

Twelve miles to Newark
and the rumbling bumps abound from here on out,
This stretch digs up ideas and visions
in all their ephemeral reflections lit like strobes
by the steady flashing of streetlights overhead
peppered with median trash scrabble & brake light blues
swimming among the faces of loves and friends
and victims and heroines,
The sounds and smells of impossible places
mix their crisp and distorted past
with those that could have been
and a present of uncertainty and possibility
strewn with pothole jug handle stop signs
and parking lot puddles of tranquility

Twelve miles to Newark
and running around the same places makes them home,
Together in them we grow, our neighbors know and share
which parts are the same and which have changed,
the stomping ground always breathing, always new,
refreshed by the rains
and the river of generations running along and through,
Some nights are quiet even with everyone hustling,
Some houses forever with darkened rooms,
Some jungle gyms rusting and overused,
Some lots are still ghosts
even with all the traffic and wild blooms,

With Twelve miles to Newark
We ride through all the shared stomping grounds
of all our brothers and sisters
working and loving along this stretch,
We ride and bump and cough and dream and hum
for our neighbors and our passengers and ourselves,
the hopeful without quitting,
the wronged and forgiving,
the steady,
the unstoppable,
the reaching out and hiding inside,
the long game sufferers and the flash pan dreamers
and all the blazing hearts with heavy heads
from here to there forever come & gone

Twelve miles to Newark
with our best efforts ahead and we can't stay long,

Twelve miles to Newark
we hum this little poem for anyone and call it a song.

For All the Anomalies

Where landscapes of cloud tops go on as if forever
giving grandness to ideas like oceans of ovaries as the
inexhaustible seeds of the coming of the undreamed,

There is if nothing else an unending possibility,
undesigned and unrealized
with unquenchable potential
and the pure perfection of anomaly,

Each and any thing we investigate is its own anomalous
invention, by the chance of ripples set in motion
or by some immanent engineering, or both,

It is entirely integrated among every other anomaly in its
universe, each inherently differentiated,
each originating from some process, some fiber,
some familiar source,
some working set of principles
with no need for regulation or enforcement,
only rhythm and evolution and fuel,

The most forgettable corners of our world are,
despite our disregard,
all born from impossible conglomerations of miracles,
from interwoven mechanisms
as yet and always to be unexplained in full.

Pipe Dreams, Pipe Dreams

So many pipe dreams,
So many just for fun, bearing nothing,
So many with so much riding on them,
So many letdowns and disappointments,
So many surpassed by the bigger dream the day brings,
So isn't it all about expectations
and are they their own negations, exactly,
So easily swept up into pipe dreams,
So difficult to resist them or dispel them
as so many symptoms of a deeper swelling,
So harrowing to carry them
but to be relieved of duty from fulfillment or eradication,
from total destruction or transformation,
So can ideas take the place of lumbering expectations,
unclasped but by the hands
that can hold the light from a flickering flame,
synthesized for their brightest bits
and implemented into the living,

Can pipe dreams live on for refinement into ideas,
Can pipe dreams feed the rumbling underneath,
Can pipe dreams coincide with weightlessness,
Can one be free and still let pipe dreams pass on by
and pass through and back to the big beyond,
Can one let pipe dreams go and not miss them,
Can pipe dreams make the will for freedom real again.

Cold Feet Blues (Get Up and Do It)

If the early bird finds his worm,
what to do but watch and learn,
Your turn, you fret, O unknown one,
begets no more, no less the burn.

Nobody Cares

You have an idea and the juice to make it real
But you hesitate or neglect it indefinitely,
Do it anyway—
The worth of your imagination cannot be known
before it's had a chance to live,

You have other ways you want yourself to be
But copy and proliferate only what you see,
Be them anyway—
You are the only one to let yourself be taken down
or teased, the words of others speak only of themselves
and there is no validation
that will ever grant you permission or satisfaction,

You are lost and finished and without an ear or a friend,
Reach out anyway and reach deeper within—
It is your job to galvanize your solidarity and spirit,
and with the substance of your being, let go,
there will be someone you don't know who can hear it,

You are outraged by injustice and politics
But leave it to the others to do something today,
Stand up anyway—
Your voice carries sound, your hands can help,
with victory or defeat the struggle is never over,
the vacancy of the sidelines makes a bubble in your place
if you do not participate in the purpose that you found,
if you do not answer the call that came from inside you.

For the Emboldened Loners

Wherever it comes from,
the compulsion to change our ways is holy,
It is our own, our most brave inclination,
One of them, some of them,
Any one at all, for the sake of something new
or to finally tackle some familiar recurrence,

Every single Self, unashamed and truthful with the air
around us when we're alone with our clear reflections,
And every size of a given group, a bonded collective,
we couples, we families, we friends,
we neighborhoods, we organizations with missions,
we with circumstance having introduced us,

In the puddles on the picnic tables
of our back porch afternoons
all is untouched and reflected,
technical ambitions fade away,
the pulse only beats to be relieved of our remaining
demons, to sharpen up and get out of our own way,

What better use for intelligence
than to identify those weights and barriers
worthy of the energy to reconcile,
and those to forgive ourselves and our parents
and our friends, our siblings, our neighbors, our associates
for all the mistakes of impaired judgment or youth
or otherwise growing pains
reaching out furiously for validation,

What better use for imagination
than to find the solution
that will right a shadow into acknowledgement,
May those memories be made good upon
to bring justice their way
and liberation from their weights,

The scavengers in our gardens
dig up the nuts they buried there before,
Every piece of unfinished business carries its final fate
for however long it takes,
suspended in a state of hibernating without waiting,
So must the pieces of us with resolutions pending
be ready and available when we finally see them,

What better commitment for the Will
than to make the transformation of the self and the world
into one more part harmony,
To join and hear more clearly that single Melody
that shines and rises,
always running steady with no crescendos,
with its inexhaustible capacity
to empower the stream and the flow of that music,

So go on, emboldened loners,
Let's go on and free ourselves, from ourselves,

What better application of the energized mind
than to guide itself right along
through all the opportunities and challenges
that define us any given day,

We will step wrong, we will hurt each other,
we will miss the chances to make good on one-time deals,
we will make good on those still open and those to come,
once and again,

Because we are the other,
no matter how far in the hole of a loner we are,
and the other is us, struggling together,

Our song is the one that runs through all the twinkling
stars and all the beating veins and pumping hearts
of all the mistaken, all the forgiven, all the seekers,
all the broken, all the invincible trying and pushing and all
of us with our ways of redemption yet to be realized,

Let's go on, emboldened loners,
our march of freedom never ends
and we never tire
and from now on we'll never go anywhere alone again!

For all the configurations of predator and prey,
Of the unlikely and the readymade,
Each with its inherent tools and talents
is built to make of this world a playground.

A Late Summer Tune

Oh please just give me some of that mystical something—

Let me stumble on some of that morning sun
shining down the neighborhood street,
that haziness of waking up with the unsleeping world
as if it had also lain like a log when the sleeping is good,
Some of that lunchtime brightness lighting up the peaks of
productivity in comings and goings,

Give me some of that afternoon peace with a breeze come
all the way from wherever it was born the other day,
Some of that sweet evening release,
Some of that nocturnal industry, that night shift
running and working while the day folks snore and turn
and dream their imaginations away,
Give me some of that juice
that turns nothing into newness,
Give me some of that rain on my face and on the trees,
Give me some of those stars burning all those years
just to sparkle sometimes in our eyes
with light that left before our world was born,
shining at the same time on all the places between here
and there and beyond and whatever else is out there,
Give me some of that stuff that scraps all my plans,
Give me some of that stuff that makes me wonder
how we got from there to here,
Give me some of that mystical something whose only
mystery is being integrated already in our searching selves,

Give me some of that mystical nothing lifeblood of our
world, that river of miracles that flows from the regular
and the plain,

Oh please just give me some of that late summer music in
the air and never let me ask again
because I am washed away with it
like the tree that reaches up forever
and will never be the seed again.

For the Lift and the Frequency

If only we could be as fluent and free
in every language of the world as in our first,
having gone and lived in the thick of the people
who know only that one,
We could compose at least one original offering
to every town from right there among them,
Some bunch of words that embodies and reflects a few
pearls from the core of where the language comes from,
For all the places through time and changes
all across this place we emerged,
Some bunch of words for all the colors and the ways
that are embedded in the people
even across the waves of their generations,
Some bunch of words if only a splash of natural justice to
the source and its transformations along the way,
Some bunch of words because the bugs will outlive us,
Some bunch of words that sound like the land around
even though the grass and dust and plants don't need it,

If only we could even use our first language well enough
to illuminate our most genuine moments
with the greatest brilliance a language can have,
If only we could read aloud an offering to the crowd,
On the back steps to an empty yard,
On the curb in the ear of your partner crossing the street,
In your living room during the afterparty,
In tuxedos one and all on the wood in a concert hall,
On the afternoon sidewalk in the city,
On a bench by the turnstiles in the station,

In the cockpit of our rocket ship with no one waiting for
us back home where the language was born,
In the driveway when the neighbors come around,
On the highway with the windows down,
In the forest when the buds open up in the morning,
Under the sheets in whispers lighter than wrinkles,
At the dinner table with empty bellies,
On a tree stump in our daydreams,

If only we could churn the essence of all that sends us off
to play or on adventures of duty into words and sounds
that would mean something to anyone around,
For the drunkenness of dreamers
imagining so much richness and beauty,
For the deepest hurt from dreams undone
and relief for a world that continues on with its day
regardless of the loss or the washing away,
For anyone who ever grieved what life didn't bring,
For closing our eyes and feeling all that is real
rising and shining inside us and all the space around,
For living out loud and rightly at the same time,
For riding the rail that lays itself underfoot just in time,
For gliding when the lift kicks in
and we leave behind the rail and the tracks and the road,
When all our words and music are good enough vehicles
for the delivery we sought all along,
The reason we spoke and sang that first time
even though the voice was not our invention,
The reason we're forever seeking that impossible
configuration of perfect frequencies
to express our best intentions.

On Our Stories

What is your story and what is mine,
for all the times we ask the air or ourselves,
for all the times we nevermind,
I can't see my story yet because it isn't finished,
Will it ever be finished or does it continue on beyond me
in the memories of others however deep or fleeting
in the convergence and deflection of paths and particles
intersecting with mine as we ricochet off each other,
Do I live again in the repercussions,
Do I ring somewhere as a wavelength in the vibration,
Does my shadow pass silently by,
Does the tail of a note find any tuning
in my having struck some part of it once,

I have seen a ripple from my presence
pass through the paths of others and nudge them,
I am one of many, no more or less
than the rolling thunderstorm would notice,
Then if my passing can make a nudge
So does that of everyone,
Every creature and every piece flowing along
with the purpose of the pinball enough to simply be,

If my story is threaded among any other
With awareness or not
Then they are as well with each other,
There we can see the immutability of everything,
And so there can be only one story,

One grand story going, never finished and never known,
Never to be fully seen by all of its contributors,
Each their own universe,
Each their own wonderment,
their own ignorance, their own perfection,
The impossible interconnected influence of their stories
is required by the running,
Each one its own, new as morning,
bringing improbable uniqueness to an ancient verse,
Each one its own drumming the pulse of some echo
set in motion so long ago, still seeming new somehow,
like the morning coming fresh and crisp
as it's always done before,
All the afternoons and evenings,
All the pastures and all the corners
spread across and tucked away somewhere in our stories,
Let them dissipate or carry on,
Let us differentiate our own,
All within the expanse of versions, of trials and of designs,
Let us not compromise on the contributions
we condone or internalize,
Let us not accept apathy amidst our confusion,
nor the strictness of tyranny for the illusion of control,

If our stories define us and fade away and continue,
Here's to mine, Here is to yours,
Here's to all the tumbling pebbles in the ever loving river,
Here's to the beauty and the blindness
and the brilliance of our stories,
Here's to our story, the familiar and the forever untold.

For Comets and Candles

Pretty ladies lace their shoestrings tight for adventure

The coronation of potential floods the disparity
between plans and blossoming reality,
where no one can tell us when to fight or negotiate,
and gravity is the grand decider of when we are fools
and when we are the wiser,
The dance floor never clears at an endless party,

Clever ladies never pace and never let a chance go by

Boredom is often the producer of venom,
boredom of ideas, the hopelessness haunted by memory,
pervasive memory polishing its shelves
where collected trophies shine with saturation,
each heavy piece of baggage unknowing of the other,
together a collective weight kept secret
by a ghostly deceiver within,
none can point a finger that we do not know this game,
As persistence for the redeeming shore is sustained,
its well grows wetter, its animal untamed,

Funny ladies need not nurse their charms, being near them
is gladness defined, if you can keep a whisper from
slipping through your hands without smashing it,

Resistance is a winless defense and though a way through
may glow with goldness, show me someone who has never
found a key with no door for it to open,

There is no estimate of worth for washing your heart
with empathy for the dearest of friends and enemies
and all the in between anybodies,
There is no bravery in disregarding
what exuberance would give to a neighbor in return,

Fearless ladies can comfort you with their jokes

When leaving a place
you can see the time flagged by goodbyes,
Let's give hellos to the crusaders
who brave unswum rivers for brilliance and good times,

Wipe one tear and blow it forward, comets and candles
are much grander than wish-making vehicles,
But to stand or soar alone through the darkness,
To carry on despite the hopes of others,
To bear the memories and imaginations
of children and old folks and everyone else
without the requirements of traditional design,
without being extinguished
for the whim of a particular gift or for a different fate.

We the Royalty

The girl made princess,
how can she endure the expectations of fairytale dreams,
But the woman made queen
to bear the light of a generation
and shine exemplary through life and age,

She is one of us, she comes from us,
How many want her to be only the dream,
How many believe the story is only what we can see,
How many prefer to ignore the source of her motivations,
the substance she offers beyond the theater,
And how many are willing to remember
that her life behind the doors is the same as ours
but for the awarding of trophies and medals
to those of us invited up the stairs,
The child smiles the same,
the marriage is alive beyond the name,
the ruthlessness remains in the game,
The temptation to make ourselves celebrities without walls
is our slippage into believing the fairytale can be contained
and played out in a bubble of our own making,
That there would be virtue in our expectations of the
same, and her sacrifice would be worth her life
if only for a moment to all generations and all nations,
She was worth it already, when she stepped through the
dream, still standing, with a mind to shine that light on
everyone, to reach out and wave at the same time,
because for her we are the untouchable,
the invincible, and the object of her dreams.

On the Roar of Woman

There is nothing that can be said definitively about all
women any more or less than can be done about all men,
We all have some defining ways to be celebrated,
but our roles are inherently ephemeral and we among the
ranks all know that none of the blanket biases are true,

One must advocate for the rights of another
no matter what the situation,
but there is a historical bend around sex and gender
and the treatment of each other,
Men must be advocates for the place of their sisters in the
ways of things if those men are to fulfill their destinies,
The fight of the woman, and for the woman,
is a noble and necessary one
to rise above the sometime in history when men thought
they could take an upper hand in living,
that they should make an upper hand out of nothing,

But the woman with wisdom, steady and true,
shows a man what is right, as she is known to do,
No worse for wear
but galvanized by the war of convincing,
Not that she must do the same as he does
but that her contribution is complementary
just as his may be to her,
And the roar of woman, to remind him it is his roar too,
Neither is more wrong to dismiss or neglect the other,
Both are made more strong
by working and loving and trying together.

Ramshackle Bliss

Maybe the grass is long, the bed never made,
the walls are softening cardboard,
the ceiling rumbles from traffic and trains overhead,
the tent blows open,
the neighbors are stray dogs who got the better place,
the rain always finds a way to sneak inside,
the windows are always broken,
the curtains are thinner than your underwear,
the hallway smells of cooking only when you're hungry,
the couch always stinks, the fire ever flickering,
for all that may be left to be fixed or made tidy,
for all that may threaten to drive the kids crazy,
for all that lacks and goes forever wanting,
for all that hides behind the haze
of the sunlit dust in the air,
If there is none of these, or more,
If you can make a home out of this, wherever it is,
then you've made a home in all the world,
waiting as it was all along,
wherever you lay your head can be missed
and you can be around any old place
with your mornings, your afternoons,
your evenings and your weekends in perfect ease,
Because the odds are it could always be worse,
and if it couldn't then the world is fully yours
and you're an angel already in your ramshackle bliss
suffering the inequity of your brothers and sisters,
with a voice to raise if not a pot for pissing.

Painting with Information

A dryness hung in the air
between the voice of my heart and I
with no reminiscent hues to confound the discussion,

We were saturated with the haze of life and decisions
and my heart balked for the faces with infinite shapes,
I reminded my heart that it alone has the capacity to know
how many waves come to the coast,
how many splinters in the timbers
or hairs on the roots of all the trees,
how many drops of blood in all the beasts,
how many primordial dust bits in the blowing breeze,
how many sprouts of grass in all the growable ground,
and how many rockstone boulders make the mountains
and how many are still growing from underground,

Not to catalog them as a data collector
and worry about the correctness of the accounting,
But to characterize the vastness and intimacy of everything
and to bring some peace to the unknowable
in its essence and release,

And my heart exploded into an immanence of Love,
Like all paints of all palates at once.

For Circus Parade Daydreams

Festivals and fairs with funny girls from all around
and able guys to follow them down,
Down at the old shipyard by the boardwalk,
The harbor lights line up shining
in the first Autumn nights of the coming migrations
and the cool, cool morning
where the smell of the new season always finds you first,
Carnivals with haystack mazes and clowns and games
with prizes all treasured and discarded, every one,
The impossible tents of the traveling show
are peppered with confetti and golden leaves
on a floor of ticket stubs and flower petals and footprints
embossed in the mud that once was plowed or untouched,

How many seasons can we see as new each time
and savor every one,
When being easy in the breeze means letting it go,
When loving is not to devour the thing,
to choke it with infatuation
and dilute the lover from remembering why,
But to let go of everything,
To run and dance and juggle and ride,
We performers and patrons of the game,
Giving names all around just to live them out,
Creating our own distractions to be suffered and shed
while we go on ahead,

What Love we have for the aesthetics of living,
The monks might say could hold us back,

But why else bother letting everything temporary go free
if not to live among this ordinary anywhere, and let it be,
To swim freely among this ocean of impermanence,
For the learning of love through endurance,
The brilliance of uncaring beauty,
The brightness of heartbreak,
The drunkenness of elation
And all of our circus parade daydreams in between.

Plowing for Seedbeds

When we ask of ourselves,
Of our loved ones,
Of our departed ones,
Of the idea of the omniscient one,
What response comes but one,
To be sure of this

Life will be different from what we imagine it to be,
Better, Worse, Both, Different

So if you find yourself searching for satisfaction,
Turn your mind to being an agent of beauty,
Turn your eyes to the cosmos of sublimity,
Offer your hand to the loving union
that brings forward a special difficulty,
the intimacy that requires one's faults and faculties
to be shown alone in the fully lit field,
To abide by the Other's habits and weaknesses
is not the truest challenge for the Self,
To abide by elucidation of one's own,
to forgive oneself and the other for noticing,
to forgive the light for shining and the shadow for casting,
Take the healthy hurt for growth alone and together,
Leave the toxicity for your elation to incinerate,
Take the surprises,
Seek to be wiser,
and Live the pledge,
Because the value of strength is in service.

We Go Driving

When the weather opens up we go driving
When the world closes down we go driving
We go driving through the wooded hills
and around the sheep farms,
past the cows lazing and grazing in grassy beds,
through the one-horse towns still hazy in the clearing of
late afternoon rains lit with the evening's coming,

We go driving around lakes with riders casting lines
and looking back at us from rafts and boats
unmoved by our passing,

We imagine for a moment those lakes as puddles
left from melted glaciers of the weather generator,
And all the rivers are runoff from the constant cycles and
systems born long before and running long after us all,
We see the lakes as puddles from mountains and airplanes
just like those on our sidewalks and driveways,
We see ourselves nicely niched in the right part
of some Ice Age, with something under our belts
and some mysteries yet to come,

We go driving with the pedal down
like a wild speck in the wind
to celebrate our invincible spinning in the blackness,
our one half snore shooting out from an impossible dream
whether or not it gets heard,

We shift in our seats around the bends and turns without
slowing down, sniffing out moments of perfect riding
just like so much unknown got aligned and resigned
to put us here at all,

We go climbing hills with the engine growls of maximum
throttle for all that is fragile and endures anyway,
For everything that makes it through the unlikely
to spin off some miracles
and then be as quickly dispatched when its time comes,
For all of us ever gone
with so much learning and suffering behind and ahead,
For all of us who build and break and build again,
Here comes you and I,
All of this so we can go driving by these island barns
in windblown plains with worn out fences
and empty benches by the roadside,

We emerged from the same seed of pure clean loneliness,
Two solitary souls going on along their way,
each meeting another of its kind and despite itself,
without reaching, finding a complement to grow with
among all the forces and gravities
this planetary cloud machine could ever know,

We go riding to show each other our incredible gifts
and our most stubborn difficulties,
To see our lives with a little more clarity each time,
To stand more assured
through the patterns of our renewal
and help each other get through it,

We go together,
For the turning to be made leaner
and the bravery somehow easier,
For those who see you as a strong and mighty woman,
they have no idea, and still I see deeper inside the
endurance of the little girl you were before you found me,
The sweet little girl who still fits in a chair like a tangerine,
who hushes for the rabbit and the deer
to stay nearby a little longer,
who hums for joyfulness like pressing a button,
who steps lightly among the flowers and neverminds the
breeze that hangs a leaf in her hair for decoration,

So when the little girl and the woman
both get overwhelmed from the business of modern living,
When she grows weary and spent
from too many hypocrisies on parole,
too many judgments without consideration or evidence,
too much neglect of goodness for a little more gold,
too many unhindered vagaries of justice,

We go driving around this little patch
of dust and trees and hills and streams,

We go driving through all the crackling leaves
and splashes of rain and snowflakes and sunbeams,
Because I found you in this labyrinth of vacancy,
And you found me,
What else is worth doing than to ride around together
through all the regular and the simple,
and to wonder about the limitless and the fleeting

and our fountain of reasons
for pushing and fighting and continuing on,

We go driving
through all the precious and all the waste alike,
because all of it is necessary,
We go driving
to remind ourselves that these lakes were once glaciers,
that these snowflakes once were at the bottom of the
ocean, that this starlight left its sun several Ice Ages ago,
that this togetherness once came from loneliness,

We go driving on the roads that once were nothing,
going nowhere, to see and feel the engine again,
and to remember that our difficulty gives us growth,

We go driving and we celebrate,

We go driving to find the new ideas,
the new tunes to hum, the new roads to hum them on,
For all the reasons that burn in our perfect vehicles,
We go driving together,
to get away from it all,
to swim in weightlessness among the breeze,
to get lost and keep going anyway,
to invent new ways to find our way home again.

A Little Holiday Poem

It always arrives before we are ready
with just enough time to orient our heads
and remember why we throw this party,
To celebrate without a care, for a cause or for none,
to devise a new surprise this year, for anyone or everyone,
to decorate and prepare
and let the rest of living be a daydream for a change,
on this day it's not cool to be above or beside it,
the only true strength is in the ability to participate,
Because we make the festivity ourselves,
we will take any reason to celebrate the living
with music and gifts and food and lighter attitudes,
A toast to those who should have come
but are unaccounted,
and a toast to those who would have come but are gone,

Here's to us, we made it this far, such as we are!
Here's to us, we promise to cross a few more things off the
list by this time next year!
Here's to us, we carry the spirit of those who couldn't
make it and so we must also drink their share!

So here's a little holiday poem for you, my dear,
not for any reasons of religion or scripture,
but to make a time when we live all those intentions,
that we make a point to celebrate and advocate
all of our appreciations,

I love you asleep on the couch
by the last light left on after everyone is gone,
or asleep on the ride home,
I love you offering something to our friends,
wrapping presents and tying bows,
I love you exasperating over everything still to be done,
I love you relaxing from the completed preparations,
I love your sadness when the day arrives at last,
I love you everywhere and all the time,
holidays or work or play,
table full of food and sink full of plates
or scraps strung together so we can say we had a feast,
I am thankful for you, being just as you are,
and for our constant reminders
of the reasons we celebrate

May we do it every day, all the year through,
and still make the occasional holiday feel special
with all the festivity that for me is inspired by you.

Birthday Poem

Once for freshly cut grass and newly planted trees,
For the swirls of particles
that make this world an ocean of color,
For the light that shines on the last of the rain,
For the leaves and hairs that let us celebrate enlightening
breezes come from high and far to where we are,
For the flight of newly found tunes we hum,
For the blood and tears we let escape
and wipe away to let us heal and embolden us,
they will break loose and we will wipe them again,
For the squinting of surprise laughter
and the weightlessness it brings,
For the pains we bring and bare and wash away
with as much time counting as the depth we care,
For the sneezes and hiccups and bumps and tickles,
For the mysteries yet to be unlocked,
For the keys we've needed and the ones we've let drop,

Again for the long grown grass and tall shading trees,
For the constant motion of molecules and strings
that keep this world forever changing,
For the current of transformation that binds us to wonder
and liberates us from the shadows of our blunders,
For the clouds that loom in the cycle of replenishment,
For the flags and branches
that rap in the winds of our turbulent hearts,
For the bitterness of unthinkable news to our ears,

For the bruises and scars we absorb and deflect
to heal and embolden us, to arise and heal again,
For the comfortless crying
and the silence of cheeks drying,
For the pains we discover and transfer and overcome
with as much time counting as the depth we care,
For the bruises and burns and prickles,
For the mysteries haunting our otherwise perfection,
For the keys we try to create and the ones we've forgotten,

Still for the far innumerable particles and their smallest
components that make us all one ocean of being,
each and every one fully integrated with the other
sharing all the particulate counterparts in one continuous
exchange of the fabric and fibers of physicality,
For the unrecordable moments of bliss
and the unforgettable impressions in between,

These are the shapes and colors of our lives,
diverting before the dead ends of our fights
and passing the times gone by from the other side
when we're going back to being friends again,
These are the spokes of the wheel,
These are the turns we take until freedom,
These are the steps to liberation, the wings of our being,

For all of this and all our dreams,
All our favorites and all our mistakes,
All of our gifts and treasures, our sacrifices and losses,
All of our concessions and celebrations,

There is no wheel the better turning,
No dinner the better burning,
No mixture the better churning than this one with you

For our giving, for our learning,
for our evolving together and glowing,
for everything we stumble on and let go,
What else but our dreams could keep us going,

Now blow gently with a wish
that only you and the candle will know.

On the Blaugrana Moving Maze

This footballing club of brothers is a puzzle in motion,
granted the artist's consciousness
with a diet of naranjas and lightning,
To observe is to marvel,
to pity the opposition in its nobility,
to see any given weakness as a fatal inadequacy,
With those glowing heads and boots among them
who go flawless like the saturated brush that replenishes
itself and cleans up the messes of the less endowed,

Eleven gilded angels would be a few too many to believe
the spectacle could not have been orchestrated in advance,
Too invincible to let remain the tension
of even that small seed of uncertainty
as chance and fortune remain baked or glazed
to give bounces and turns in favor of the fateful,
But the forever building, the forever searching,
as one measured rush of water
mixed to eleven parts daring
and love for playing the game
balancing on its crest
the weightless marble of impervious right,
running through a changing maze
and every drop finding its way,
Liquefied crystals pulling labyrinthine walls
that shift to balance their improvised architecture
and they with elastic ideas twist or carve or cut in turn
to reveal the current underneath all along,

They feed every drop through the eyes of needles
as though the impossible way was always the plan,
and collect together to double back
and make the maze again,

Their admirers are tireless and forever unsatisfied,
forever devoted and starving to see the next ways,
how they unfold and contort
and how they will unravel the walls
in another masterpiece
of the collective and merciless dismantling
For its own sake,

In the beginning, you know, for sport,
And in the end for its redemption.

Those Old Japanese Poets

Slipping through thick misted evenings among the pines
with the sap smell and the cool silver moon shining
through all those needles and cones and seeds,
the birds all around
pecking or flirting or sleeping,
and all the moss, Evergreen

Soft cloaks and able sandals swishing and gliding
among the rocks and rivers and pines
or motionless in nonexistence
or ready to continue on,
by the rock mountain, Gleaming

Those old Japanese poets,
always a full eternity away from where we meet them
and always immediately with us in their reading

When we walk with them, we remember,
they were not old when they wrote those poems.

On the Road in Our Bones

Long have we moved from here to anywhere
when the unknown road is the only way,
Strong is the tradition
of those having to set out for another home,
to remake the entire mark of survival in this world
for that chance of a new one to bring more openness,
more opportunity to work in fairness,
to rest with peace and to taste some enjoyment
of the everyday living, of a life fit for growing,

From war, from abuse, from the crossfire,
from restriction of those essential spiritual freedoms,
from the reasons anyone would run to the last option
that is the Road,
the Road without songs but of the traveling kind,
the Road without joy,
the Road without familiar faces waiting down the line,
the Road without knowing what chance for loved ones to
survive what comes along,
the Road with difficulty, with growth, with despair,
with soul shaping challenges and luck,
the Road with those stories of life and no fanfare,

Let us help to welcome you back to living in the world,
to resume your lives in pursuit of peace
and enjoyment of life itself,

If we accept that the ultimate and ideal goal of human life
is to support the spiritual liberation of each person,

Then it is necessary as a collective
that we orient our minds and decisions
through our hearts
to reliving the fundamental needs for survival
with as much depth and expanse across our Kind
as our dreams can hold,
An unending effort never to be fully accomplished,
itself with room for all the dimensions of social living,

Let us be brave for a bigger justice to be forged by human
hands and all the related activities of jobs, politics,
education, struggles and victories,

For this it is necessary that our efforts be built
around a universal agreement,
One so natural and obvious
that it need no dissection or argument over its pieces,
rather that energy be spent
navigating the ways and mechanisms of its advancement,
One not so unspoken that its Will and its Harmony go
neglected and forgotten as trends,
but we keep the correct simplicity
of the child's knowledge of what is right and fair
and the lighter and better manner of being,

For all of our injustices and our wars,
if the majority of our momentum
leans to the support of each other,
we can achieve whatever is available
from our necessities and dreams,

What pulse then beats in our veins
but the single rhythm
of a collective driving and hitchhiking of ourselves,
What pulse rides on the waves that carry the boats,
What pulse puffs out in clouds of dust
from all the footsteps on the road,
What pulse rings with the desk bells and fog horns,
What pulse do we make airborne today,
What pulse beats in the ways of our places in this world,
What pulse of those on the road
is different from those who can help lighten their load
from the journey anyone would concede
had their situation been the same
as those who had to leave.

For America the Forever New

The New comes only from the growing,
The New comes only from the moving,
The New comes only from the middle way of the road
running ceaselessly ahead,
always underfoot and always ready,
The New is a continuum forever being born,
forever born from what came of it before
mixed with what energy willed it into something more,

Generations thread the needles of their days
with first times for everything,
their predecessors having done the same
and their followers in the wake
will face the same challenges
with all that seems different about their turn,

Who doesn't want a collective identity for their country,
a prevailing purpose bigger than personal interests,
a shared concentration of skills in the direction of a society
made bigger by personal considerations,
We fight to design the shape it should take,
the architecture that would keep us in meaningful debate
and remain afloat from the weights of the selfish and the
corrupt, that would welcome practical solutions ringing
true with their problem reasons and informing the way,

The harder partnership of our measured steps
would be the more equitable and productive
for probability's fates,

Each of our steps would be conceded
for the sake of what must be done today with an eye to
build some stone for tomorrow's better foothold,
to wrap more coil for the bounce
in tomorrow's springboard,
How else really but with the stepwise progression
of the collective, the treading together,

The question centers on the direction of the weathervane,
the prevailing intentions that give structure to a
hardscrabble architecture of collective policy and practice,

Is the purpose to endlessly lift the most fortunate with
promises that their scraps will fall eventually to the masses,
filtered through measurements of growth rates,

Is the purpose that an entire society of brothers and sisters
should support this dice game and sustain it
with hope of miracles for their food
and only hopes of miracles to unlock their pursuits,

Is the purpose for the more fortunate to help support the
less able, all with work to make a home,
with the rewards of achievement blessed with
responsibility to a society of brothers and sisters,
every one, that the impulsive temptation to protect every
crumb, which would destroy us all, be tempered by the
greater belonging with the world, that respect always be
mutual between the exceptional and the rest,
everyone doing their best,

A society of brothers and sisters
whose nobility is to live the greatest celebration
of liberty and freedom, which is to help others while
supporting one's own and to do so gladly as participating
in the collective life of the current generation
and of those to come,

There is value in taking stock of the state of things,
when all the voices find the most disparate of walls among
them, when the listening becomes sickening and isolates
the voices with similar tones to band together in echoes
that drown out the others from consideration,

What stock do we take in this fresh century,
but to see as our predecessors have done
the aging out of the cold minds and hardened hearts
with hope that the innovations of those younger entrants
bring a brighter beacon of liberty and prosperity for the
people at home and abroad, somehow in their way, that
their swell would carry the greater portion of momentum,

Because the aspiration of liberated living for the individual
must be the most worthwhile endeavor of the many,
bringing recognition that all individuals are anomalies,
some will always fly ahead, some will always remain the
slower, some will strive to help them, and some will always
leave them behind,

It is the unison of the collective
among the necessary diversity
that must not fail and slip away
with the speed of the reckless,
but remain measured and purposeful
for the good of the brothers and sisters
of which each individual is one,

Born or brought from circumstance and work
May every hand reaching out
find its complement reaching back,
May every shoulder slumping down
find an arm with empathy,
May every worthy Will find a benefactor,
May every beaten spirit find its sea legs,
May every victim of a careless system
find its way through to improve the gears,
May every qualified voice exercise its responsibility and its
right to register its ideas in the offices of service or voting
or otherwise contribute to the every day struggles of its
brothers and sisters in humanity,

What stock then do we take with these trends of liberty,
That the rights of the new arrivals and decent intentioned
be the same as those with roots long entrenched,
That the disproportionately endowed be shamed by the
collective to more purposefully acknowledge its place and
participate responsibly in its neighborhood,
That the light of living as One shines in all corners, with
none to escape or hide, and to balance this social justice
with the necessities of personal privacy,

That the lessons of thoughtfulness and humility
be the ones to endorse for those growing up younger had
the more experienced a chance to do some part of it over,
There is a New America whose pulse beats drums
underneath diversions and distractions,
it is the rhythm of its intentions, the river of its purpose,
it is as precious as a whisper and mighty as the tide
and only made up of the ones who stand up, speak up, and
take the rights of the broad collective as their side,

May their cause always find courage and friendship
when facing attacks from selfish skeptics
or the misguided or the uninformed,
May it always find vigilance for some semblance of justice
by whatever length fate requires for the arm,
May their generation's gasp for air
be one more for the record books,
preserved only for the challenge and the succession,
and fuel the momentum
of the next wave of freedom fighters through their days,
May their generation learn better
to separate favorite beliefs from best public policies,
May their saviors, every one, who washed the feet of the
desperate, not be attributed incorrectly with advocacy of
the trickle down table crumb architecture of the selfish,

Take stock of yourself America,
your progress rings with brotherhood and sisterhood
through the fog of flashing lights and words,
Your progress seeks attention
for the desperate and the helpless,

Your progress rewards the well endowed
and requires their success bring responsibility
and participation in its democracy,
Your progress calls out the deception
of the ill intentioned,
Your progress demands the measured hand of
consideration for your brothers and sisters
in America and across humanity,
Your progress has had its fads and cast them aside
and hungers for substance among bubble gum culture,
Your progress has a mind to straighten the ways of
business and humanness in a globalized social economy,
Your progress has less doubt
that the remarkable is possible!
Your progress has sharper tools to mobilize the
mechanisms of awareness and action!
Your progress is learning how to discover itself
and trim the fat from its shockwave blast
of technology and saturation!
Your progress demands the reasonable and responsible be
allowed to operate with freedom and service!
Your progress demands inventiveness and compassion!
Your progress demands solutions!
Your progress is the New Lifebreath of the America some
world fell in love with long ago!
Your progress hungers to remind the world
that America is a land with its mind bent on freedom and
equality of rights for brothers and sisters of every shape
and color one and all!
Your progress is in your hands!

Your progress is the New America!

You are the New America!

The New America
has rustled and tossed and turned enough to rise,

The New America
has rustled and tossed and turned enough to rise!

The New America has fidgeted with its bits long enough to find eagerness and rise!

The New America has widdled away its ornaments of distraction and has no choice left but to rise!

The New America
is ready to make its dream into reality and rise!

The New America
welcomes the hard road to a more proud humanity!

The New America
welcomes the hard road to a more decent humanity,

The New America
is in all the brothers and sisters under the flag,

The New America
is in all the brothers and sisters under the stars,

The New America is ready once again to be a harbor for
the weary, for the dreamers, for the new beginners,

The New America is a new beginner, open your arms,

The New America is a new beginner, open your arms!

Open your arms to the victims and the strugglers!
Open your arms to the thugs and the astronauts
and the homeless and the helpless and the bizarre!
Open your arms to the wronged,
Open your arms to the strangers
and the different colors of your neighbors!
Open your arms
that they may find a warm body to embrace,
Open your arms that another may find yours
to help each other run the endless race,
Open your arms and heart and mind to slide through
those fundamental human ideas we know to be right and
true and worthy of the new morning!
Open your arms and rise!
Open your windows and doors
to let the breeze come through,
it is the stream of brotherhood and sisterhood
and liberty and togetherness and freedom
that makes our old infamous America ring again
with the tune that made its first beginning
from a desperate dream into this living thing,

Open your arms to let the New America grow in the
direction of oneness with each other the world over!

Open your arms if you want America to live in tune with
its original intentions a little more today and tomorrow
than before,

Open your arms, New America, you must know yourself
as a true harbinger of unbiased opportunity if you are to
renew and galvanize your identity once more,

If you are to remind yourselves, and the world,
why it is worth being America at all,
but for the way of a decent humanity
among this chaos survival neighborhood of a world.

Defending the Enemy Within
(or Confronting the Soft Spots of Self-Regulation)

I will look after myself,
you must trust me to look after myself,
to be both productive and responsible at once,
I don't need any help from you
and you cannot tell me how to look after myself,
Yes we live together despite my constant daydream of
perfect isolation from anything suggesting inconvenience,
Yes I should be left to design my own way
without your interference,
I will do what I believe is best for me,
the roadkill is the necessary ends of my ambition,
Some of the roadkill is a natural accident of learning and
living, the suffering I did not know or mean to cause,
Some of the roadkill is a purposeful disposal of my
perceived barriers and detractors,
because the living is hard
and I am the wheel before I am the victim,
if I think twice then I introduce a weakness inside
that will undermine my fireball catapult path,
All of this because I believe I am alone
and whatever I do is gained by my steam alone,
this is convenient for saving the energy
of acknowledging the endless interconnection,

So I will set my own rules
and I will find ways to subvert any mechanism around me
that I deem to be unnecessary,

I will judge which are the good
and which are the inefficient,
I do not make mistakes
and I will decide whether to repeat them or not,
I will make successes
and I will determine how to preserve them or not,
I will give when I win, a little bit, and I will take,
All of this by my own legislation, by my own indignation,

If I am a person, the machine will churn me or ignore me
based on my interference with the turning gears,
and I will absorb the consequences of my own jurisdiction
in as much time as takes to be noticed and counted,

If I am an organization, if I am a gear in the machine,
nothing will churn me but the long arm of evolution
in as much time as I have resources to buy,
with as much distraction as I have resources to rhyme,

Where is the balance between friendly consultation
and the tough love of external discipline,
the guardrails I didn't consider,
the balance between liberty to be as I see fit
and the worth and the effect
of my intersection with the world around me,

Where is the difference between what I think is best for
me and what in fact may be,

Where is the balance of cost for those dealt wrongly by my decisions today, they without enough voice to correct the currents I set in motion during their lifetimes,

Where is the evaluation of the guardrails that protect me from the collateral casualties of my self destruction, my celebrated unquenchable thirst for ever increasing expansion and growth,

Where is the wakefulness and maintenance
of the antiquated chains of watchers
long fallen asleep at the watch post,

What is the value to the collective,
of which I am a drip and a drop, of the constant cleaning of cobwebs from the closet and the vigilant watch of a supportive and productive watch at the ready,

It is that the arm of justice, of what is right by the collectively acknowledged whole of a society despite some marginal pursuit of a single entity, be as responsive as the wheel of adjudication can bear,

It is that the collective be educated to appreciate that investment in a more refined system of responsibility for today's and tomorrow's best interests and efficiency,

It is that the well-being of a society not let the production of stuff supersede the quality of its building blocks,

That half a world of people not suffer their living
conditions by the selfishness of the unconcerned,

That the everyday necessities not abide the hoarding
admirals who are fully detached from consequence,

That if the bedrock and the structure should fall into ruin,
the enemy within not be excused to walk away,
shrugging by the dust of the avalanche that his position
will be fine and the rest will take care of itself,

That any price upon everyone else is not worth the
wildness of one individual's unhinged ambition,

The value is that the self-concerned who looked after
themselves alone be held accountable,
their responsibility is as well to those who struggle under
the long arm of justice, their responsibility is not only to
those who contributed beans and bones to their account,

The value is that our interconnectedness be an asset to us
all, that we invest together in our best efforts of self-
administration,

That we not let our world go careless with itself
making decisions from our soft spots of selfishness,
laziness, corruption, and abuse.

Tomorrow's Fate

For all the imaginations of our exceptional extinction,
All the possible ways we might impose a terrible violence
upon ourselves, sweeping our future clean,
Are we more likely to trudge through
an eventual undoing,
an inevitable becoming of nothing
in methodical pitter-pat drabs of sprinkling doom
played out for generations,
the last of us without a real clue of how our dire situation
had ever come to be from so long ago,

And what good to focus on our ending, and how,
There is no end for us now, there is only today,
no meteor, no missile, no virus, no eruptions,
just the now with a salvation of tomorrow,

So everything we do can be for the moment's judgment,
to keep the place alive and clean,
to reach a height and extend a hand,
because tonight we all bed our heads,
Tonight we lie and let dream the minds of wonder,
and tomorrow what we left today is all we'll have for
ingredients to scratch and scrounge and save in vain,
There is no keeping but for tomorrow's use,

Tomorrow
We find what's been swept under and cast aside,
Tomorrow
We'll only have what today we managed to abide.

The Environment Argument

In the end
In the ever blooming beginning
In the forever now

There is a reason for taking care of our own home,
A reason that defeats all personal beliefs,
all institutional claims,
all mysteries and all disagreements of science or politics,
A reason that encapsulates all good reasons and all of their
oppositions and still rises superior in its simplicity,
A reason that flies frictionless with the underlying spirit of
any prophet,
any God,
any atheistic no-God,
any agnostic maybe-God,
any enlightened everything-God,
any enlightened nothing-God
using any definition of the word God for any of these and
any homemade system of any brain and heart walking
around that imagines how anything came to be what it
seems and why and what that means for people,
A reason that can give us confidence even with our
admission of humility in the awareness of the impossible
Mystery embedded in our existence,

The confidence that comes from Choice,
Our decision to roll on a momentum of our own design,
The choice to be a part of our world rather than
pretending it is separate from us,

that we might continue the adolescent phase of squeezing
every last coin and drop of utility out of our home before
discarding the garbage and by-product of its mining until
we live only among the consequences of our spending,

The choice to be a steward of our little corner,
of our stoop and our range,
to keep it in mind when designing our mining plans
because we are the predecessors of tomorrow's situation
and we choose to send a more responsible and habitable
momentum through the generations,

The choice of accepting our ability to make peace with our
home and have playfulness in its appreciation,

If our ways are born of Nature and alive by them
then there is no difference between us and where we live,
Our power then lies not in illusions of entitlement
but in applying our gifts and our uniqueness
to thrive in service of our irrevocable oneness,

This premise is the only one with a universal staying
power that is harmonious through our ages,

In our maturity may we find peace,
In our peace we may find freedom,
In our freedom may we unleash the creativity of our
glowing hearts and brains all over the place,
And our inventions designed to be in line with this,
unhindered by entrenched interests of selfishness,

Made for today and for the generations ahead
because we accept the challenge of our exceptional nature,

And so
We are stewards,
We may be the best of our kind the universe all around,
We may be the ones who would look ahead and smile by
our behavior in this place where the impossible was here
long before us and we are the most improbable of it all,
We may be emboldened by the ability to make our own
choices,
We may be strong enough to make them in harmony with
the world that allows us to be here at all,
With the world where we can perceive and appreciate
everything that is born and grows and transforms
throughout the depth and breadth of our observations and
our wild imaginations, and beyond them,
Beyond them in the great unknown we often dream of,
the amazing possibility
of always another surprise up ahead somewhere,
another kind of newness still to be discovered,
All of it resides forever in our home,
All the newness awaiting us is already alive in our home,
Everything lives forever in our home but those things we
alone destroy that could have been preserved,
If we would not, one of us, destroy our most loved people
and things for a couple more beans,
What difference then in letting anything be treated with
less preciousness or attention than what we give our own.

Oh, the Sleepless Shore

Zero gravity beyond the sky above,
One lone star passing with every turn,
One bright star of life, may it forever churn,
Two searching seagulls
gliding above the waves without touching,
Three shouts of castles smoothed by the flooding,
Five pairs of great ship honks of the coming,
Eight feet of the racing and hopping and burning,
Thirteen beats of sleep
for the breathing without dreaming,
Twenty-one pebbles and shells for discovery,
Thirty-four sand crabs and jellyfish in the morning,

Countless visitors
for the place with no permanent residents
but the waves and the sand grains
shaped by the Wind and the Moon
while all the rest may come and go.

For the Interference of Daydreams

We dreamed of Paradise, the one we knew,
shining and vital with the fullness of exultation
and easy wisdom of our otherworldliness,

Our dreams took form as dust blown to a clean floor,
each grain familiar and indeterminate,
but together, a sparkling cloud,
a hint of a future we might already know,

We are never so young,
We are never too old,
If we have seen changes in the shapes of our dreams,
they were blown as dust into a cloud by us,
And if our dreams in total have flown into a gone
goodnight, there is one that remains,
the center of the core, the source, untamed,

Our hearts, on the whole, do not fulfill every day,
and the dreams somehow dissolved are sent on their way
when the cosmic broom pushes through
and the vortex is mixed with the dust of the floor,
A euphoria shines within us, erasing our pain with its
blindness, if only to light our way for a moment,

What remains is familiar and indeterminate
and sparkles like a dream that awakens us
so we can chase another one down and see it through
or make it new,

There is nothing so easy,
There is nothing too hard,
If we will ever be wise, there is one thing only,
We know the best is to stumble across the floor
that sparkles in the dust cloud of our dreams
with a friend at our side if we can,
all the rest aside,
And be a friend to them as well,
all the rest will be alright.

Notes on the Necessary Future

In all the visions of the far reaching future
if they are not ash and scum and gray and piss
then they are sterile and efficient and blind,
but in between the desolate and the sanitized
we can see the design of tomorrow
which is that expert of today,

We can see the oldest and the simplest of human
inventions enduring in function,
their origins as caricatures of evolution's tireless intention,
the fun of all their forms and fashions
burn bright in arrival
and are already forgotten on departure,
We can see a couple riding bicycles along the roadside,
We can see rethinking old problems from different angles,
concepts and execution coming full swing,
We can see the necessary and the impossible
meeting in the middle,
We can see the cornerless, compact, standard issue original
and its wildly modified self in every color,
every size, every possible option of material and
configuration such that the thing lives only by changing,
And its existence reminds the observer
of the infinite invention of human imagination,
by the user, for the user,
that the use of things will be defined by the necessary,
and the necessary defined by the performer,

Scale the personal customization to everyone, impossible,
Keep it from anyone who seeks to perform, impossible,

The future of a proliferating population
must include in its direction a focus on closer intimacy,
At least one prominent ingredient bent on harmony,
Enough room for the liberated to experiment with abilities
and create that which serves the greater purpose with its
function as the user chooses its form,

The aesthetics of what may come
is left to the designers and the dreamers
focused forever on utility and cohesiveness,

What is the future but our projection mixed with fate,
A reason for today's losses to live again in purpose,
A chance to steer ourselves the mighty middle way,

An idea to light up our imaginations
for the ever possible refinements,
the ever running for a more adapted and more inclusive
view, and a more universal consideration for our more
relevant applications of all that we can do.

The Frog Riddle

A valley is filled with trees,
green and steaming and pungent,
There are many clearings scattered around,
clearings for breezes to air out when the winds sweep along the valley floor, and to receive the fruits of storms cast off the mountain wall,
In one clearing some branches hang above a pond
that is gloomy when doom sets upon it
and glitters with magic when its gloom is doomed,
There a frog sits on a log in a pond
gazing across the top of the water and wonders
Which lily pad should I hop to and sit upon,
Which other log in what pond in another clearing should I set out to venture on,
Some are wide and long with lots of room for stretching,
Some are fat and full with softness for padding,
Another one is the greenest and another is always moist,
As the frog cannot decide which is best,
So it sits and wonders through all its days
Asking the moon and stars in the deep of night,
Asking the clouds and birds and the sunlight,
No answers from the moon or stars or galaxies beyond,
No answers from the birds or trees or shining sun
Until one day, resolution arrives with ease, and the frog sits in a new spot doing frog things in frog ways,

Which did it finally decide was best
to spend the rest of its wondrous days?

Our Lives of Realized Dreams

The secret wishes we make come true
when the music fits the scenery
and we pull ourselves through,
to live like that all the time
and never see it among everything else we're trying to do,
Like the afternoon sun that catches us once in while
by surprise, some house or barn lost in a field,
some hazy horizon in the opposite direction,
some disappearing driveway waiting by the roadside,

Someday or never, to know we've already been the thing
we imagined ourselves to be, or better,
It never felt the way it seemed,
the being was different from what the hope could see,
except the essence of its original wish,
To live the object of a daydream is to set it free
and never taste the feeling that made it be,

And we, making some dreams with purpose and some
despite us, which ones our passion, which our weakness,
All our fate, all our footsteps,
For those to come and those long blown away,
For all our wishes, how many do we realize and see,
how many do we live, and how much difference in
between but for the moments of openness and clarity,
Like when an idea from the deepest depth comes,
we never speak these secret wishes, often unseen,
but we can live them if we can let them be.

For Patience without Waiting

The branches part in breezes from afar,

The will to do what has brewed and now bubbles with
readiness is stolen away with unguarded secrets,

The dance of the exposed shoots oases of freedom,
relief and opportunity in what was only darkness,

On deciding upon a turn of fortune,
is it all some premonition or unknown predilection
churning out the workings of a plan already crafted
and somehow running itself through,

Or does our nose lead us everywhere
by the smell of our divining rods stretched out just ahead
for that which may come from the unseen road,
also somehow derived from you,

Way beyond the gaslight and the windmill,
awakening waits for the self-ordained explorer,
like the breeze that arrives to part the branches overhead,
inevitable, eventual, and available,
awakening waits to make good on all that starvation

but for the long long long release.

Beginnings and endings are blended together,
Failures are fortunes of growth,
   the endured is let go in peace,
Victories are springboards,
   the weights are released,
The wheel of absolution is in motion, Let's go,
We hold the keys, We make the tools,

Let's go! Let's go! Let's go!

A Rescue Mission Proposal

Let's go on from here, right now, this afternoon or evening
or morning, they are all the same,
Let's go on and leave our reasons home,
On a deeper mission with no glamor, no attention,
On a deeper mission with only our conviction and our
vision of harmony with anything and everything,
clear and easy as we are when we are united together with
the invincibility of openness,
Not a mission of whimsical inspiration or adventure,
Not a mission of tasks and rewards,
A mission whose only threat
is what goes missing from staying home,
what growth ungrown from fear of failed rebellions,
Let's go do what we will
with the responsibility of acceptance
and the freedom of vulnerability!

Ours will be a mission of resilience and utility!
Always in the surrender a new transformation!
Always in the transformation some gift of the unexpected!
Our mission is a river of opportunities to begin again,
to abandon or sustain or adjust the heading we're on,
To take control of our rudderless souls!
To guide ourselves like snowflakes in tornadoes!
For all our struggles
isn't it some eternal easiness we're looking for,
But decisions stick fast in our structures
and the illusion of comfort in perceived control requires
our blind affirmation of why we made those decisions,

Our mission will leave no corner of us alone!
We will face those decisions that have stuck in our heads!
We will master their underlying architecture!
We will bend every turn of the circle into lines!
We will take every chance to learn the shape of our path,
To see it and speak it by name,
To drink it in and swim in its rays,
To taste the essence of our discoveries of what churns
inside and underneath,
To make the spirit of our observations live again as fuel,
To apply the insight of revelation to our lives and endure!

What does it take to remember the reasons at the core,
How can we stretch the gem of that liberty all throughout
the endless galaxy road
through all our gears and all our tools
So all our buttons and levers glow with our learning souls,
So all the magic and mechanics of the turning underneath
goes on with the uncaring and the profound,
That we go on like comets in all our beauty bound,
To rescue the bug without breaking its legs,
To let go the light of the day,
that it remains all through the night and into the next,
How do we realize the real life of a dream
so it can be replaced by experience,
When to start, when to stop,
When to dig in and fight forever and when to let go,
Let's go on a mission to answer all our questions,
To graduate from questions whose futility we expose,
To search and discover and never run out of new ones!

For the Intergalactic Inside

The blood in the buds of adventure blossoms with vessels
and filaments and supernovas that light the fires that break
and open our hearts,

The night at midnight flourishes with repose & delight, its
darkness and starlight autographs our hearts with
luminous secrets whose temptations loom as gas and dust
precursors to something in our imaginations,

The light in our eyes
is brightened by the windows on our rocket ship ride,
We are welcome for a little while anywhere
as we roam around anointing the tones of the universe as
music and using it to reveal the rules we grew inside to
fool ourselves that the mystery is not also ours to ply,

Vanished into oblivion they go,
each of our rules found and forgiven in fateful blinks,
We trace their origins to the fearfulness of exploration, and
their release to the inevitable victory
of daring to meet the unknown,
And so we decorate our weaknesses with ornaments of
doom, that they may never slow us down again
in our pursuit of peace with the cosmic broom,

The comet that flies never burns the same path twice,
We may pave the roads of gravity's might
but our orbits remain unique and related,

We roll along the fabric of fate by the nature of our being
and in rolling set our bells to swinging from their
wondrous fulcrums,

We ride, dispensing tones that plummet like noble rebel
drops in a limitless bucket whose want for walls lets the
waves of our voices in the vacuum ripple on so far as the
sound and the will of the call,
Always destined to dissipate, to go absorbed or unheard,
Born of fire and realized by our imaginations,

We can hear the sound of freedom within our cores
and it glows so bright
we can follow our hearts throughout the night,

We let the vortex of our orbit blow heartwings into flight
to ride on the currents of the blood
that makes our adventures somehow worthwhile,

To birth the buds that blossom with our struggles and our
victories, and to swim in the gravity and the stardust
that unites them all.

Heuristics Are My Prayers

When the roots of wrath begin to burn,
When the anger wells up from deep inside,
When the head swells and the heart races with all the
impatience and frustration of my insatiable temper,
When I can taste the metal on my tongue,
When I can see my ugliness in the eyes of others,
Then I am a voracious eater of people,
Then I can turn anything into garbage and dirt,
My tools are sharpened always and they don't determine
their own use, they are ready when I reach down,
My mind and words together can turn anything into a
shell of itself in my dance of destruction and waste,
I am the grand venom with my fangs at attention,
Even if justice or virtue is my defense
I can still fill myself with a ravaging filthy anger,
There can be roars and rants with no room for mercy,
But all the spectacle a temper can muster
cannot last forever,

In the aftermath, the full shadow of this anger falls idly
beside the piles of ashes, proud of its muscle and power,
The aura of that anger stands visible in front of my very
eyes, encapsulated by its limits as if in pure physicality,
With the temper fully blown, my heart then sees what
remains as the smoke clears, and it softens automatically,
despite me if I am still annoyed,
as a witness of itself in turning the lens around
with no thought stream running anymore

only silence and observation of the face of my creation run
through all the senses,
I breathe the aftermath as if drowning in pure air,
I can see the manufactured fireball of all my
dissatisfaction, the sour fruits of misguided industry,

And every time I realize, eventually,
That the anger doesn't bring any benefit
to the situation that had enraged me anyway,
The fury and destruction only weakens me,
Letting the full energy of a toxic reaction loose
is not really a demonstration of strength or power,
but a lack of mastery of the most basic impulse in myself,

Some of our instincts are purposeful and well placed,
Anger from injustice is necessary in modern humanity,
Other automatic reactions such as those calls for action or
beauty can be guided purposefully
with our own power and virtue,
But there is no better craftsmanship of the self
than to recognize those seeds of impulses
bubbling up from underneath,
To be prepared in the moment to guide that energy
into whichever direction my masterful brush deems best,

I will make no mistake to presume in the future
some anger will not plant its seed and shoot up again,
This anger is mine, and I am strong, so the path without
steps leads nowhere and no step forward can be wrong,

Standing unafraid and unashamed
as a witness to the feeling that welled up and overtook me
is my opportunity to see its true colors and its roots
through the fog of distraction
beyond the ego's armor standing guard for the ego,
I will face any vision of the inner workings
and call them out by name

Eureka! Eureka! I see you!
There are no shadows here inside!
Eureka! You are exposed by the light that shines!
Eureka! I see your ingredients!
Eureka! I see your origins and the path that leads to here!
I am the driver of this vessel and I will find your source
every time and there will be no room for you!
I will plunge my hands all the way down inside!
I will dive to the bottom and then do it again!
Now that I have been to the source I can never forget or
neglect to work on you like a surgeon!
You will return but I am in the long game!
It is true that anything is possible and I will outrun you!

There will be no more wasting of energy on the objects of
frustration I'd created myself, for my own distraction,
with all the mirrors of misdirection,
I can do whatever must be done along the way,
Every answer I seek will emerge apparent, eventually,
having been ever-present all along,
Or the premise of its question will be revealed
as absurd or unnecessary,

There is no barrier to mastery of my own inner workings
but the vigilance I apply to empower those ideas,
And so I breathe a little prayer to the air,
a simple vow to my future self
that the world may crumble and fall and I will stand tall,
that my lighter side take the wheel from now on
with my heart as its rudder,
this heart that is just a vehicle
for the infinite expanse of wonder it wields,

Because I am the fool that others have been,
the fool that others will be,
the fool that moments ago, of all good people, was me,
And I can unlock a better judgment
by the grace of my own commitment,
I can make a project out of this mound of clay,
I can try and I can chip away, and why not,
Is there not some hapless comedian in there anyway,
Am I not more powerful than imagination,
Have I not been adequately humbled already,
Open to loving and trying, and humbled again,
Are we not more able to shape ourselves with our built-in
tools such that a vow with no promise but to itself
can serve as an embedded reminder to recognize the
shadows and levers of distraction and calamity,
To trigger the Will into applying its lessons,
To tickle away the boring and the grave,
To try, above all, and to chase those brighter versions of
ourselves that we see in our visions and daydreams,
that we wish for in our whispers of desperation.

On the Anatomy of Liberty

What does it mean to be free,
Does it help to imagine our own deathbeds,
Sitting alone without visitors
We can see through the light from the window
All that we have done,
All we have been,
All we have become,
All we have dreamed and not done, or chosen otherwise,
None of this a confessions, only the truth we have known,
There beyond the window in our room
We can feel the open potential of the unknown,
What might lie ahead that we have not yet become,
All we have not yet dispelled or neglected or grown from,
This is the illustration of our path, This is who we are,

Are we not free to accept all of these,
To see ourselves and let it be,
To allow as they are the shapes we trace in this eternity
however small or brief, as our turns so far,
Do we not have the same chance, each of us then,
To taste the ultimate dream,
To start from this moment our lives of freedom,

Are there tools we need to navigate the way forward,
First, to Be,
comprehensively and weightlessly,
it is the sweetest and the most human aspiration,
made from what makes us,
Then some tools without name or measure,

crafted by our souls and polished by the road,
To continue on and make the most of the way ahead,
A way to Go,
to Go,
to Go!
to Go!

The right way for each of us
with Thoughtfulness,
with Vitality,
Nurturing the recipe of that imminent or elusive liberty,
There is no catching, no holding,
no finding without losing,
There is, in freedom, only release,
only recognition and release again,
There is no baggage in freedom,
There is no baggage in the Being,
What else do we need to know!
Let's go! Let's go!
Let's go on a journey inward
with all we've seen and all we've heard
with all that's going on along and all that's gone aside
with our determination and imaginations free to shine,
Anything can come on along, the whole world over,
With all we've been and all we've dreamed,
This is our chance to toss the ropes and float away,

All of our adventures start and go and end inside,
So let's go on a journey with springboards of our souls!
Let's go on a journey inward
to devour the anatomy of our liberty and Go, Go, Go!

At Home on the Open Road

What are the tools of the human spirit and mind
granting access to expression in concept and craftsmanship
of simple and perfect design,
What are the buttons that put blindsides and bends
in the road of our own growth and illumination,
All of the levers and traits that make us unique
are also the walls of our customized labyrinths
to understanding the true nature and ways of our world,
The mechanisms for liberation from the turning wheel
must be built in to our system already,
Liberation must be our highest aim, each of us,
and as a social animal we must grow and lend those tips
and abilities to our riding partners and neighbors,
We must recognize the shadows and symptoms of what
smells like a tool towards enlightenment or liberation,
And we must detect those weights and chains headed
down, however contrived or familiar, and share them,

None can go it alone, all the way,
One can only go it alone, all the way,
How to more efficiently identify the weights
and the keys of liberation,
How to most purely play one's role in the open field,
The results of this pursuit are only for the person,
The methods and ways
include all those swept in the same current,
It is the Will and the Attitude and the Walking of the path
that define the work to be done,

There are attitudes of the seeking that can shed the weights of prejudice and hate,
they come from the anger of dissatisfaction,
born in every expectation that we manufacture to hedge our fears of uncertainty amidst a world with no answers,

But Ideas
and Risks
and Bravery of Spirit
and Willingness
and Mindfulness
These are the replacements of fear and expectations,
With these we can see more clearly the work around us,
We keep purpose only with effort,
We keep promises with full commitment,
We keep preferences with the latitude of humanity,

Hard enough, this mission, taking a lifetime or longer,
How easy then to dismantle and abandon
some weights and chains at least,
If only to walk with solidarity of one's own spirit on this mission, where then can such endorsements
as racism, inequity, selfishness and falsehood lay claim,
To dig deeper into the fabric of one's opinions,
To seek understanding as a mechanic of the soul,
To dig through and lighten the load,
Ever alone, and never alone
In this nothing impossible cosmos where we live,
And if that's not enough what else have we got to do.

For the Other Ones

An entirely open environment
provides the broadest spectrum of opportunities
for those creatures grown up with a capacity to seek
or create meaning amidst their survival,
In ours there are as many opportunities for action and
meaning as there are possible connections among axons
and electrons in the circuitry that sparks in the dark,

With a broader network of circuitry available to draw on
than all the other blood-pumping beasts,
We with more intricate abilities carry an inherent
responsibility to swing that double-edged sword with
purpose, to study, to revel in joy, and to pay attention,

So gather the Philosopher, the Poet and the King,
the brightest and mightiest of Minds and Wills and Ways,
Can they figure a way to feed all the people,
Can they explain why all the people will never be fed,
Can they marry the drive of the exceptional
with the right of the challenged to make true brothers and
sisters of neighbors and strangers,
What ideas do they bring to reveal harmony
among disparate beliefs about the nature of things,
Can they inspire the anarchist to purpose
and the conformist to action,
Can they proliferate the peace of Zen nothingness,
Can they move us along with any or all of these charges
down to the last detail,

What are the principles that can fit into any framework
and facilitate practical living in the Zen no-framework,
Do they recommend we be an adult of a civilization,
That we remain playful,
That we be stewards of our collective home,
that we take care of it, and each other, as best we can,
That there is no time,
making it impossible for us to waste it
or to arrive in bliss or rightness too late,
That there is no power for a person enforcing their own
ideas, but in shedding the idea of having any power at all,
That the past may only appear better than the present only
from fear of its seed, which is Mystery,
the same that makes the future appear better
than the past or the present, which is Dreaming,
and together these create and sustain reminders regarding
our scope and our place in the scale of things,
Do they abide that we will always fight,
That we will always draw lines between us,
That we must always try, regardless of success,
That we must account for the inspired, for the wasted, and
for the difficulty of doing right,

So for those growing up with the capacity to seek meaning
amidst our survival,
only the humble, only the giving,
only the unaccounted can show us what is alright.

This One Is

For the unnoticed paths of the passing runner,
For the unattended space alongside each step
that adds up to a landscape,
For the persistent unseen but by the hitchhiker's glancing,
For the runner and the hitcher themselves unnoticed,
For the pedestrian picking a leaf for brotherhood and
sisterhood and sharing a place in the ever unwitnessed,

Does she know she is picking a piece of herself,
Does he know he is as left alone as the passing parts he has
never paid attention to,
Do they know there is only the relentless road,
the head up and the heart in rhythm,
the vision aligned with a breathing mind,
the fuel for growth from what comes along,
the light and some synthesis and the growth again,
How often is it that we are the thing we saw as separate,
that we are what we shake away as the other,
that we are already in the place we are looking for,
that we are the leaf, the branch, the trunk,
the tuft of grass, the puddle and the shadow and the
stranger lost and found at once in the incredible vastness,
that we are roadside and the landscape and the path,

We are the oddity and the other, already blended,
With only a faint veil of shade to fake our differentiation,
we sustain the illusion only by our laziness,

We are each our own in shape and color,
And still underneath, a mixture of one another,
Before and after,
Forever and ever,

This one is for recognizing our connectedness,
For absolving any fears of similarity,
For dissolving illusions of peculiarity,
For the odd and normal and their impossible difference,
For the ever loving Sight that pervades every corner,
For the runner gone by and the pedestrian picking leaves,
For the hitchhiker and the rider,
For the fighter and the helper and the left behind,
For the story of the ignored that leapt ahead,
For the unknown road that never waits,
For the untread path we each must make.

The Pilgrim's Whistling Tune

Of all to be done before switching dimensions
let me ride correct between destinations,
Measure my ambition against its purpose,
inform my decisions with intuition
and sharpen my reason with imagination,

The patterns and the process of being
are woven among intentions and surprises alike,
and they of the fabric turned inside out,
Swim through the skies of emboldened days
and float with silvery eyes in the dark,
For all the fireside dreams
that engrave themselves and cannot be,
some to struggle for and some to set free,
the turns make the road all around me,
the road reconciles my feet and daydreams,
and I with a hand in the wind for direction and futility
lift my chin to smell the seasons and the horizon,

All the tangible is all the fleeting,
what waste in its treasuring,
what nutrition in its weightless appreciation,
The sweetness of what should be
is sealed tight and brightening,
The images of what could have been
are so desperate and illusory,
The chances that it will not be
are so frightening and liberating,
What hope to spare us all from the cruelty of ignorance,

What hope that we wade in the grace of the unknown,
What purpose guides our trajectory,
What purpose churns our artistry,
What breeze blows in from the last of the long rain,
What ease puts me to sleep before I hit the pillow.

Window Bridges

The lights and the breeze and the currents underneath
give the river its shimmering ways
all through the day, into evening,
all through the sparse sounds of the slumbering dark,
and all through the steady pulse of bustling days,
Too early for dawn, too late for night,
only the unseen is the stirring,
all is unheard but for stumbles and intersections in the
space, the breathing and the scurrying and stumbling,

Waking before everything else brings realizations and
intentions, memory of previous aspirations and
illumination of the difference,
The rising and going and rhythm of carrying on brings
acceptance of the inherent and moving forward,
When these impressions of one's fateful path
are not the same, which are digressions
and which the keen clarity underneath,
To go on in the current state
seeming always to be chasing,
To go on with the current day
being always of the making,
And to lean in for some path in between,
taking in the unexpected coming,
shaping one's own direction in the drumming,
What is the balance for a modern person
of survival and accommodation,
of sacrifice, of the terrifying,
for a chance at thriving,

How many parts are the things we bring,
How many ingredients that just fall in,
and the stirring, the stirring,
to dispense the steam of the extra,
to condense and refine and be left with the clarified,
the boiling, the efficient, the bright and the burning,

How much is all this wonder,
this suffering, this industry,
simply a vehicle.

With a Mason Jar in a Corner Store

We can see backward in some distorted way,
figuring what we were back in those days, from today,
with some air of that perspective
as through an artist's eye,
We can see the people and the places and the things,
We can send them off or write them down or leave them
be to germinate or reconcile another day,

        Can we see forward as much the same,
            without the experience yet
        to let us know we've done so
or to recognize anything at all with any certainty
        and let those visions come through
            as ideas and impressions
to feel embedded lessons in time to make decisions,
            to live in some distorted way
        should we find ourselves there some day,
        and the meantime we can spend
drawing pictures of our own futures and fates,
wondering which will be and which are bait,
and calling them all the science fiction of today.

Gold & Blue & Orange & Silver & Gray

Walking along the melting snow
I can see back through all the gone days
of childhood and beyond,
These late winter afternoons have always been the same,

The sunny ones with water trails
and the water goes wherever it can,
the only places it could,
and we stroll hand in hand,
a real or imaginary perfect partner in the world
breathing full and clear with every beat and every step,

We can lift our heads and peer into the low sun dusk
and appreciate a sparkling sadness
from our love for this mystery place,

We can be alone with peace and cold noses
in these translucent afternoons
and tap our fingers through the frozen bubbles
ahead of us in the air,
Our ideas hover among them
with the meandering bits & flakes & leaves & bugs
taken up by the wandering breezes, our purity floating up
there with our opportunity to make a masterpiece,

We alone can create this single one of many
no matter who or what or how or whatever tools or none,

We make the ingredients and each of us can and must
make of ourselves a masterpiece, to fully imbibe our
pursuits of harmonious and purposeful perfection,
In fact it is our duty and our destiny to do this,

We define our own perfections
in the being that never ends,
even on the cold lone gray winter afternoons
as on the bright sharp blinding blue winter afternoons,

We are fresh and new in the ever creation and
transformation engines of our Beinghood!

Zen!
Zen!
Zen!

Zero!
Zero!
Zero!

The world from living brings no more than we do!
Sha-zam and A-la-ca-zam!
The weather was made to come and go!
We can live as many lives as we must in one turn we go!

May all the winter afternoons always be the same,
and may we always be new
come wind and sun and the route.

On the Forever Transforming

An Autumn afternoon in the suburbs,
cloudless skies and angled sunshine,
the first of the leaves come down
in the greenest of the grass since Spring,
the Memory stings and the Imagination is let to play,

A Fall afternoon on the lawn under the trees,
the quiet kind that makes anything possible,
Even for a loved one gone to sit here with us today,
We sit appreciating the work of the Season,
We sit dreaming of the work yet to be done,
We sit wondering what our world looks like from all
dimensions and about the transformation of matter
on every level,

We wonder about the unaccounted elements in the
impermanent body, the lost weight of the expired corpse,
the passing of quantum bits between dimensions
and if the lost ones are the weight of the proliferated
carriers of the Something,
and if it will ever be again as before
some semblance of an enduring essence
floating freely in timelessness
or dispersed as integrated pieces among many new ones
like those little bits blown around from exploded suns,
like those little bits collected over millennia among planets
and canyons and ocean beds
and asteroids and mountains,

like those little bits collapsed from all those leaves come
down and left to become part of something else,
Always working, always moving, and sitting,
And rising again, right on time.

On Living Again

Who doesn't love to wonder about reincarnation,
If it isn't the case that we go through just the once,
To have lived before and to live again,
For always until whenever as something each turn,
Floating in the breeze or according to a prescribed fate,

The common thread across all possible vehicles,
always human or varied among beings,
some configuration, with or without progression along a
food chain or consciousness gradient,
Living at last with a chance to sort one's self out,
To live in peace through liberation from the shackles,
To leave the cuffs dead in a heap
fulfilled of duties no longer needed,
the empty bracelets of color, direction, and proclivity,
In this condition I never pray, but for one thing only
To have enough time
to live consciously my own liberation and freedom,
to taste the peace that is tasteless with being,
I may have forever to do it,
But to live it in this time,
To be the turn that sets all others free,
I may have some single, finite no-reincarnation chance
with a clock stopping
solely by the mechanics of physiology,
I may have some combination of factors
taken from all the ideas of this and more,
the unthought obviousness yet to be seen,

May I find the pieces that hold me back
and recognize them in the moment
as growing into ideas, behaviors, and being,

May I turn this whole journey
into a wheel of grace or goodness,
for all the people and things I'll be fortunate to see,
whether or not we ever cross paths again.

Architecture

I am riding on a train
birthing innumerable imaginary universes
spinning off straight from my heart, from my brain,
from the lightning that strikes where the static collects
among some clouds of dreams
between what lies outside beyond the window
and my eyes as I am passing by,

I am conjuring up from nothing the churning blossoms of
ever-blooming rootballs of tomorrow's doing
in the glistening sunshine of the hovering mist of
weightless thinking and wondering,

All is crystalline clarity with blended edges blurring
between realities of the making, like mixing paints in the
puddles of valleys shrouded in steam from the motor that
runs like a drum dispelling beliefs, the clouds in the valleys
sparkling from the breaths and stars of the forever
exchanging of the interconnected everything,

I am one with the rails,
Our wheels are singularly focused,
From something whittled however into any whatsoever
we ride entwined with the exploding fractals of our
imaginations, the fruits and patterns of our visions are ever
deepening in symmetries of sameness somehow making
new things through us, our accidental inventions,

All along the train ride
my daydreams deposit me at any point beside the tracks in
the greatest pit stops of opportunity and freedom,
Drop me off at any one of those strange places
composed only of pure potential for the passerby
and every one a home for the locals and the wildlife,
The impossible clearing in the forgotten woods,
The neglected factory of yesterday's supply chains,
The solitary water tower monitoring rooftops and parking
lots or the backend of any old neighborhood,
Wherever I hop off and land would eventually become
another launch pad just like these train tracks,
like the water drops on the daydream windowpane,
Just another customized runway like every place we find
is made to be, the solid ground and the space between,
all at once, these pieces of intermingling ideas and
memories are melded into wholes,
into translucent and luminous boat sails,
they are from visions of what could be,
of everything we've seen and lost
and hoped for and grown from,
of all the compositions and tunes
that ripple from our wave machines,
They are shimmering pictures of our turns on the train,
What luxury to spend a while imagining impossible
universes and how to make them real sometime,
What else in this dream of dreams
could lay the tracks up ahead in time to ride upon,
What designs from the borderless conductor,
What freedom to ride with the ever dreaming engineer.

With Gas Station Sandwiches

Where loose change makes few melodies
from the sparse availability of it
but for in pockets and purses of the passing lives
who count and apportion it here and there
with decisions and dreams of some impossible departure
to leave this place and burst in some new scene all blazing
with the radiance of the emboldened and born again
with new shoes,

Where loose change pays for lunch
familiar names in the same old places
look beyond the immediate landscape
where few roads provide avenue for arrival of new faces,
Brother, Sister, Alien, Neighbor,
All are the same any given day,
One becoming the other
with long histories of transfiguration or no histories at all
but for the ephemeral transaction,
All stay put or move on,
All reach down to hunt for the needed fuel,
All reach out for access or answers or for reaching's sake,
All come,
All pass,
All look out on the land around, the lights surrounding,
Letting in and letting go
the impressions and their absorption,
Getting up and getting out
from processing particular bits of the musical chaos
into ideas, commitments and digressions,

And we sit here in their tumult and in their wake,
We turn parallel lines
into a single perfect pocket in space-time,
We two coins given grounding and liberty by Gravity,
seeming to us to be exactly outside and apart,
An audience for none,
We are an audience of everything,
as if it were possible for our pause to be real and true,
That our songs and our stories and our greatest go-to jokes
might be relieved of duty for one beat of the Drum,
That a moment might be dived in fully immersed head
and all and drank down full without exhaustion or hunger
for another ounce of anything at all,
To never remain and never be restless,
To stretch the stuff of this existence without touching it,
To appreciate the wealth and wonder of it as we seem ably
made to do, and to swim in that forever cresting wave
just one moment longer,

But lunch is done with the inevitability of its becoming
and legs get woken with heaviness for the going,
The excitement and resistance of resentment
rise and yield in rushing sentiments
that welcome us back to the river and the road,
and from our moment in the middle of all things been and
coming,
We go,
From our perch among the borderless rainbow spectrum
of things included and left alone,
We go,

For our opportunities to turn the disregarded into news,
We go,
For chances to reincarnate hopes of trying again into little fleeting justices among the things we've seen,
We go,
For all the chances to have been something else,
For all the options consolidated into the only way we could have been,
We know,
For lunch being done and loose change spent, We go,
We go,
For the Will that sent us on and brought us here,
For the Rhythm that makes it so,
For the Source that fills up everyone and everything,
We go,
to Burn,
to Learn,
to Empty out with the industry of Wildness,
to Glow,
and to Fill ourselves back up again,
We Go!

For All the Passing Stoops

Front porch lights twinkling through the trees
like stars among the forest sky,
lighted doormats of familiar or unknown universes,
Each with the depth and breadth of a world itself,
Each the simple point estimate of its presence,
Each of them and each of us, passing by the other
to intersect someday perhaps, or never,

There is enough in a night's ride
to open an entire mind's eye,
enough to pierce through the clouds or confusion,

So much inherent connection and perfect intuition,
to see the singular We beyond the I,
to remind us of our Oneness,
Each of us with our parts, each of us the power of our
contributions and our potential,

With all of this to balance easy,
all of this light to mark the darkness,
all of this might for our paths, for our wills,
for our unbound essence to let shine as lanterns on the
path in the deep dark jungle night.

A Oneness

I lift a bug from a puddle and blow a little hurricane
to make the breeze it cannot bring,
Bent wing & busted leg, we injured, bird and beast,
we heal sometimes or move on at least,
Our psalms are often unsung treasures,
unread whispers colliding with the silence
that would but could not have been,

There is no better way than to bend the knees,
no more a gift than to go it strong,
History is gone, outlasted by every next day,
and growth is the path
that can handle our pains in mystery,

Who could call it luck that the hard road to goodness
will forever go on with invincible vitality,
to see all doings of inherent or necessary treachery
outdone,

I take the turn that makes me,
to lift a bug from one fate and set it free
and hope through my bones
that I have left the cleverness to the skeptics,

There is no virtue, only being,
but for the skeptics a virtue to frown on or aspire to,
The skeptics of freedom, I will always be their enemy
and wish that upon them good graces be,

Pointing in the crowd
to reveal the many other faces
of the one the finger finds with reverie,
and it's me,
I am the bug,
I am the puddle,
I am the hurricane
and the wings beating again
I hear the hum of everything around me,
the blood of us all shared forever through transformation,

And so says Nature

I am the world you adore,
I am the world you ignore,
I am the world you are looking for,

I am the budded branch
with a button and a lever
to deposit my seed on the back of the bee
when he come to gather some sweet stuff inside
and fly away to spread it around
and help make more of me,

Now and again, when the season bring the honey,
Birth and doom devoid of me, Now is my eternity.

Indivisibility

This is where everything comes from
This is where everything goes

All the pieces of everything
are dancing in an unending exchange of ingredients,
We can see it in the immediate lifetime,
when the seed survives and grows
and dies to become fertilizer
because the new cannot come forward without food,
We can see it beyond ourselves
if we unbuckle our minds from the boundaries of time
because the materials of our homes
were once the growth of something else,
And all of it before that was fire and water and stardust,

This is the breathing of our universe,
the forever rearrangement of its fundamental bits,
the seed that becomes a baby or a tree,
the baby that becomes a friend and neighbor,
and the tree that becomes a home for generations of
creatures and a provider of shade, or a beam or paper,
All of our food comes from something else,
something of its own whose story ended in its use,

The story of each thing comes and goes with its witnesses
and everything disperses itself into something new,
Everything comes from the ingredients of the other
eventually,

Because this is where everything comes from
and this is where everything goes,

We planted ten trees last year where seven others fell
And the wild growth shoots up from the disintegration of
all the leaves and seeds and fallen trees of long ago,

The dust from deserts blows across oceans to become the
nutrients of distant jungles that would be nothing without
those sandstorms,

The instructions to make more salmon are embedded in
the needles at the tops of pine trees that line the rivers
where those fishes journey a lifetime to make more
generations of themselves, those that don't make it become
the food of everything around that river tomb, and those
that do become the same thing too,

The animals built to chase and those as much to run,
One of them always wins at the expense of the other,
They are made of the same water, the same grass,
the same proliferation of engines ignited by sunshine,
Neither is completely outdone as they become each other,

The people built to hunt and those as much to study,
Those to make ideas real through the magic of invention,
and those to make inventions live through the music of
their labor, sometimes they can work together,
They suffer the same weather and hunger and fate,
They depend on the same underlying structure,

They find their roles among the same community
that survives and thrives because of them both
and despite either one,
The supporters and detractors of their favorite ideas would
find no springboards but for their differences,

Every system of coexistence
weaves its threads beyond itself
among those of everything else it intersects,
There is no separating where something comes from
and where it goes,

If there is no destruction of the fundamentals,
If there is only transformation by rearrangement of the bits
that make up any of our ingredients,
Which can be singled out for exclusion,
Which parts can we ignore or ruin without poisoning
ourselves and triggering mutations of our world,
What pieces are left that will not be missed from some
treasured development yet to take shape,

When none can be separated from the other,
Everything we have come to appreciate and enjoy
as witnesses and stewards of a little corner of this universe
shares its fate with the place we make among it all,
And our future depends on its connection with everything
that made our existence here possible in the first place.

One Last Song for the Mystics

I fight on the line between wishes and dreams

Let the gleaming visions of impossible situations flow
through my imagination, not of any success or heroism,
just the clarity afforded by some fleeting enlightenment
guiding my magnificent vehicle through perfectly
illuminated circumstance,

Let the light of my eyes brighten those of anyone around
and theirs mine, sharing pockets of untenable bliss just
beyond the gravity of Time, those precious weightless pure
experiences where the Living swims in the same place as
crystallized premonitions of ideas,

Let the best ideas be gone and never hoped for again
but the framework of my heart and mind be always ready
to fill itself again with the immediacy of that euphoria
bounded only by its own levity,

And I just wise enough in face of a subsequent Thought
not to dirty it up with some desire of any sort,
Even that it last longer or spread its grace to another
or come around again to remind me of the oneness of
everything that surrounds and saturates us
and offers the chance to abandon the barriers of wanting
any more than the liberation of living in realization of our
connection with the miraculous unending already.

We in Our Sea of Stardust Milk

An ocean of lights over our farms and towns,
Which ones are stars and which are satellites,
The faraway suns are the ones that twinkle
like your eyes and your smile, my dear,
So let us hush from wasted breaths
and let the comets burn in final gasps
as we wade and splash in our sea of stardust milk.

For Those Flying into the Day

We over the stretched and full or barren,
Into the dissolving glow, the forever coast,
Suspend even our most persistent dream, the one that
remains when others have been dashed or dismissed,
and amend our fears with preparation or silliness,

We lay the way for acceptance,
to let come what may as we stand among the skeptics,
for the freshness, for the chance that it might,
remaining vigilant in our judgment
when the admission or the unexciting is the right way,

Still we go on long enough to wander through its milk and
take for its fuel what it was or why,
But for now just to be sure, and weightless, and loving,
and renewed, to go with blackness at our toes or heels,
Always through, remembering without clues that
the clearest path is kept inside, ever in the making,

So let us then go flying headlong and sure-born flying
right into the day that leaves questions and guesses burned
behind or saved for later,
We already hungry and running the pace
to find the day just in time,
With our surrenders and our offerings
and all our wishes donated to usefulness,
Our best way is always still just up ahead.

Sweet Days in the Fold

The living on through suffering,
so common and recognizable as witnessed or felt,
How bemoaned, how lamented,
How celebrated, how heralded,
How rarely regarded by others but the born gentle,
How terribly shared, how wonderfully eased by others,
How necessary to minimize the cycle
and realize our potential,
How we struggle to keep it distant or chase it away,
How we hate it or savor it
and hide or transfer it to company,

The fight to get on through and to liberate ourselves
carries us through every day,
We acting out collectively all the ways to drag it around,
stretch it out, or turn it into something else,
Something new,

Once in a while to stand at the top of a wrinkle in our
encompassing tapestry and appreciate our place,
our path with so many gifts along the way,

Thanks to the special middle ones
for making this regular life in this anywhere nothing place
more interesting and worthwhile,
Thanks to the fearless family members or companions
for singing through the oppression or poverty or hunger or
hardship, with all or some or none of these,
for joking with us through our struggles and dismay,

Thanks to the ones who sit with us in precious times,
Thanks to the ones who get up and play,
Thanks to the ones who walk with us through the worst of
it all without complaint, and let us walk with them,
Thanks to the regular,
Thanks to the plain,
Thanks to the extraordinary parts of everyone,
Thanks to the wild ones, the silent ones
and all those in between,
Thanks to the fun,
Thanks to the irreverent,
Thanks to the unsatisfied scientists in us all,
Thanks to the searching hopeless stubbornness in us all,
Thanks to the curious,
Thanks to the hilarious,
Thanks to the silly and the serious
and the loudmouths and the punks,
Thanks to the voice in the deep down gut in us all,
and thanks to those who don't let it drown,
Thanks that the suffering is temporary enough
for us to turn it into strength,
Thanks to the imperfect road
Where our music is worth all those notes
And our stories are worth being told
Through all our sweet days in the fold.

All the Poems

1

One Little Victory in Eternity	3
Notes to Welcome a Dawn	7
To Glowing Ghosts in Living Dreams	9
Meteors for the People	11
The Human Identity Mixology	13
For the Invincibles	15
Hmm Hmm Hm	17
For Witnesses and Wanderers (And Those Who Don't Love You)	19
Only the Necessary Sentiments	23
The New Memory, One for the Weary	25
The Bringer of News	33
The Ego Protects the Ego	35
Admission &	39
Forever Adolescence Blues	43
For Those With Brains and Backbones	45
Practice	47
No Revelations Tune	49
For All the Anomalies	51
Pipe Dreams, Pipe Dreams	53
Cold Feet Blues (Get Up and Do It)	55
Nobody Cares	57
For the Emboldened Loners	59

2

A Late Summer Tune	65
For the Lift and the Frequency	67
On Our Stories	69
For Comets and Candles	71
We the Royalty	73
On the Roar of Woman	75
Ramshackle Bliss	77
Painting with Information	79
For Circus Parade Daydreams	81
Plowing for Seedbeds	83
We Go Driving	85
A Little Holiday Poem	89
Birthday Poem	91
On the Blaugrana Moving Maze	95
Those Old Japanese Poets	97
On the Road in Our Bones	99
For America the Forever New	103
Defending the Enemy Within	113
Tomorrow's Fate	117
The Environment Argument	119
Oh, the Sleepless Shore	123
For the Interference of Daydreams	125
Notes on the Necessary Future	127
The Frog Riddle	129
Our Lives of Realized Dreams	131
For Patience without Waiting	133

3

A Rescue Mission Proposal	137
For the Intergalactic Inside	139
Heuristics Are My Prayers	141
On the Anatomy of Liberty	145
At Home on the Open Road	147
For the Other Ones	149
This One Is	151
The Pilgrim's Whistling Tune	153
Window Bridges	155
With a Mason Jar in a Corner Store	157
Gold & Blue & Orange & Silver & Gray	159
On the Forever Transforming	161
On Living Again	163
Architecture	165
With Gas Station Sandwiches	167
For All the Passing Stoops	171
A Oneness	172
Indivisibility	175
One Last Song for the Mystics	179
We in Our Sea of Stardust Milk	181
For Those Flying into the Day	183
Sweet Days in the Fold	185

Acknowledgments

Special thanks to KS who shares all the growing and despairing and dreaming and everything in between. Thanks also to MOD, AL, KR, SPM, THW, JP and JS whose brotherhood and sisterhood moved me immensely. And special thanks to my family, I was listening.

About the Author

Henry Cunningham lives in the northeastern United States where he enjoys working with tools, conversing with wildlife and leaving pennies in parking lots. He is a poet and a scientist fascinated by the illumination of the ordinary and its inner music. He is pretty sure that everything, and nothing, is ordinary. *The Geometry of Freedom* is his first published work written and assembled over many years, finally, just for you.